Juan R. Sanchez Jr.

1 Peter

*Living Well on the
Way Home*

GOOD BOOK
GUIDE

6-Session Bible Study

1 Peter For You

These studies are adapted from *1 Peter For You*. If you are reading *1 Peter For You* alongside this Good Book Guide, here is how the studies in this booklet link to the chapters of *1 Peter For You*:

Study 1 > Ch 1-2   Study 4 > Ch 6
Study 2 > Ch 3-4   Study 5 > Ch 7
Study 3 > Ch 5   Study 6 > Ch 8-10

Find out more about *1 Peter For You* at:
www.thegoodbook.com/for-you

1 Peter: Living Well on the Way Home
A Good Book Guide
© Juan Sanchez / The Good Book Company, 2016.
This edition printed 2025.

Published by The Good Book Company

thegoodbook.com | thegoodbook.co.uk
thegoodbook.com.au | thegoodbook.co.nz | thegoodbook.co.in

A CIP catalogue record for this book is available from the British Library.

Design by André Parker and Drew McCall

ISBN: 9781802541472 | JOB-008040 | Printed in India

Contents

 # Introduction

One of the Bible writers described God's word as "a lamp for my feet, a light on my path" (Psalm 119:105, NIV). God gave us the Bible to tell us about who he is and what he wants for us. He speaks through it by his Spirit and lights our way through life.

That means that we need to look carefully at the Bible and uncover its meaning—but we also need to apply what we've discovered to our lives.

Good Book Guides are designed to help you do just that. The sessions in this book are interactive and easy to lead. They're perfect for use in groups or for personal study.

Let's take a look at what is included in each session.

Talkabout: Every session starts with an ice-breaker question, designed to get people talking around a subject that links to the Bible study.

Investigate: These questions help you explore what the passage is about.

Apply: These questions are designed to get you thinking practically: what does this Bible teaching mean for you and your church?

Explore More: These optional sections help you to go deeper or to explore another part of the Bible which connects with the main passage.

Getting Personal: These sections are a chance for personal reflection. Some groups may feel comfortable discussing these, but you may prefer to look at them quietly as individuals instead—or leave them out.

Pray: Here, you're invited to pray in the light of the truths and challenges you've seen in the study.

Each session is also designed to be easily split into two! Watch out for the **Apply** section that comes halfway through, and stop there if you haven't got time to do the whole thing in one go.

In the back of the book, you'll find a **Leader's Guide**, which provides helpful notes on every question, along with everything else that group leaders need in order to facilitate a great session and help the group uncover the riches of God's light-giving word.

Why Study 1 Peter?

Here is a letter written to churches like ours, about a time such as ours. Peter's first letter is one we need to read, treasure, and believe in our day, because the post-Christian societies many of us live in now are very much like the pre-Christian society in which Peter's 1st-century readers lived then. Here is a letter for today.

Like the Christians in Asia Minor (modern-day Turkey) to whom Peter was writing, most of us don't face universal, state-sponsored persecution at this time—but we are encountering the reality of increasing hostility toward anything Christian as we live in a culture in which we are likely to be discriminated against simply because we identify with Christ.

We need Peter to teach us how to face the reality that following Christ and obeying what he commands makes us different—we are aliens and strangers in a foreign land. We need to learn how to endure unjust suffering in a society where Christianity is unwelcome. We need to remember what the identity and purpose of our local churches are in communities that see them as irrelevant. We need to learn how to live with joy and hope and love when we are mocked and maligned and misunderstood because of what we believe and how we live.

And in order to live like that, we need to be reminded of the "true grace of God" in which we can, and must, "stand firm" (5:12).

These six studies will excite you, reassure you, and challenge you about your life now, as Peter shows you how to live well on the way home to your inheritance that (unlike everything in this world) is "imperishable, undefiled, and unfading" (1:4).

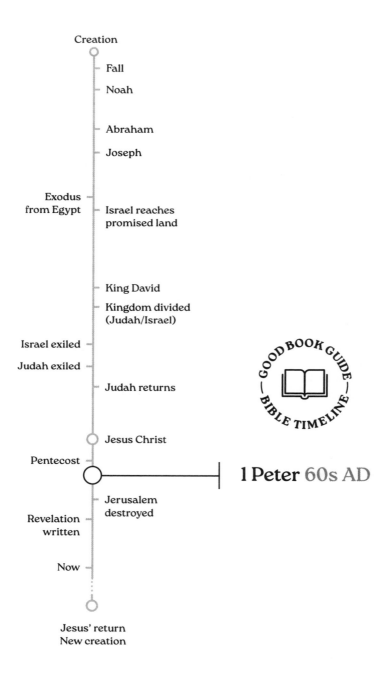

Creation

Fall

Noah

Abraham

Joseph

Exodus
from Egypt

Israel reaches
promised land

King David

Kingdom divided
(Judah/Israel)

Israel exiled

Judah exiled

Judah returns

GOOD BOOK GUIDE
BIBLE TIMELINE

Jesus Christ

Pentecost

1 Peter 60s AD

Jerusalem
destroyed

Revelation
written

Now

Jesus' return
New creation

1

Certain Future, Joyful Present

1 Peter 1:1-12

Talkabout

1. What do you expect the Christian life to be like between here and heaven?

- What makes you answer like that?

Investigate

📖 **Read 1 Peter 1:1-5**

DICTIONARY

Dispersion (v 1): scattering; a word often used to describe the Jewish people who, after the exile, lived all over the Mediterranean world.

Sanctification (v 2): the process of setting apart; here, it means the Spirit enabling people to trust Christ and be saved.

Sprinkling with his blood (v 2): in the Old Testament, a sacrificed animal's blood was sprinkled on the people to show that the animal's death had made possible their forgiveness.

2. How does the apostle Peter describe the Christians in what is now modern-day Turkey whom he is writing to (v 1)?

    E _____

    E _____

   • What does this tell us about how Peter wants us to view our relationship with God?

   • What does it tell us about how Peter wants us to view our life in this world?

3. What have the three Persons of the Trinity done for each Christian (v 2)? Put each phrase into your own words.

4. What has "the God and Father of our Lord Jesus Christ" done for his people (v 3-4)?

5. How could Peter's first readers—and we—know they would reach this inheritance (v 5)? Why is this encouraging?

Apply

6. How do these verses encourage us to live for what we will have in the future, rather than what we could have in our present?

7. In what areas of life would thinking of yourselves as "elect exiles" change the way you think, feel, or act?

Getting Personal | OPTIONAL

Does the description of Christians as "elect exiles" comfort you, discomfort you, or both? How, and why?

In what areas of your life do you need to stop compromising and start living as an exile? Are there ways in which you are living as an exile, and need to remember you are elect so that you keep going?

Investigate

📖 **Read 1 Peter 1:6-12**

8. How is it possible—and right—for Christians to rejoice in trials (v 6-9)?

9. How is this different than how the world links trials and joy?

10. How are believers who live after Christ's death and resurrection in a privileged position compared to...
   • the Old Testament prophets (v 10-12)?

   • the angels in heaven (v 12)?

Explore More | OPTIONAL

What did the Spirit do in Old Testament times (v 11)?

📖 **Read Isaiah 52:13 – 53:12**

- How does this prophecy point forwards to "the sufferings of Christ and the subsequent glories"?
- Why is it a privilege to read it now, after Christ's death, resurrection, and ascension, rather than to hear it as Isaiah's first listeners did?
- What else has the Spirit done (1 Peter 1:12)?
- Briefly share how he did this for you.

Apply

11. What stops us from greatly rejoicing during "various trials"?

- How can we unwittingly discourage fellow Christians from rejoicing when they suffer?

- How can we consciously encourage each other to rejoice in these times?

Getting Personal | OPTIONAL

What trials are you facing right now? What grief are you experiencing?

You do not have to ignore it or seek to belittle it; but neither must you despair in it or be crushed by it. If you have trusted in Christ, God is at work in your life, and he will not waste your suffering. Keep trusting in Christ; keep loving Jesus. Remember the living hope you have; remember the inheritance you will enjoy; look at how God has guarded your faith through your trials; know that God is refining your faith in those trials—and rejoice!

In what way do you need to apply this encouragement? Is there someone who needs you to share it with them?

Pray

Use verses 3-5 to spend time praising God.

Pray for yourselves, and those you know who are facing "various trials," that those difficulties would show you the genuineness of your faith and that your certain future would enable you to rejoice.

2

Loving Christ by Loving Your Church

1 Peter 1:13 - 2:3

The Story So Far...

We are exiles in this world, God's elect people, traveling toward our amazing inheritance—so we rejoice through trials, as they prove we have genuine faith.

Talkabout

1. "I love Jesus, but not the church." Have you ever heard anyone say something like that (or thought it yourself)?

   • Why do people have this opinion?

   • Do you think it's justified? Why?

Investigate

When life gets hard, we look for someone or something to place our hope in—to right our lives and give us what we most need.

📖 **Read 1 Peter 1:13-21**

2. Where is the Christian's hope to be (v 13)?

3. How will setting our hopes here change our thinking and our actions (v 13-16)?

4. How does Peter motivate us to live in this way?
   • v 17

   • v 18-21

5. Choose one or more of the following problems that we may identify as being the biggest problem in our lives: poverty, singleness, illness, boredom. Then identify…
   * what that might cause us to locate our hope in.

   * how that would influence our thinking and actions.

   * How do verses 17-19 help us to have our "hope … in God" (v 21)?

Apply

6. Why is it liberating to set our hope on Jesus' return?

- Why is it hard to keep our hope there?

Investigate

📖 **Read 1 Peter 1:22 – 2:3**

7. How does Peter compare and contrast the way we are brought into a natural family and the way we are brought into God's family (1:23-25)?

8. What is the great "family characteristic" we are to grow in (v 22)?

- Read 1 John 4:7-11. How does our Father both show us and motivate us to grow in our family likeness?

9. What has no place in God's imperishable family (1 Peter 2:1)?

10. How do we grow as members of this family (v 2-3)?

Explore More | OPTIONAL

📖 **Read Romans 12:9-21**

- What kind of love does Paul tell us to have (v 9)?
- What does this look like in practice: in how we treat other believers and in how we treat those around us?

Apply

11. What does "sincere brotherly love" for one another look like in practice for your church? Would a newcomer to your church describe your relationships in this way? Why / why not?

12. "I love Jesus, but not the church." How would you use 1 Peter 1:22 – 2:3 to show someone that if we really love Jesus, then we will really love his church?

Getting Personal | OPTIONAL

Are there any ways in which there is a mismatch between the love for Jesus that you profess and the love for other believers that you show? Do you need to change your attitude or actions?

How do the truths of 1:18-21 motivate you to change??

Pray

Give thanks:

- *for the unchanging hope that comes from knowing God's grace.*

- *for the holiness of God.*

- *for the new birth that you have been given, and for the goodness of the Lord that you have tasted.*

Pray:

- *that God would give you a real desire to be holy, as he is.*

- *for growing "sincere brotherly love" among you. (Use your answers to question 11 to shape your prayers.)*

Share how you struggle to "put away" the sins Peter mentions in 2:1, and then pray for one another about these things.

3

The Greatest Building

1 Peter 2:4-12

The Story So Far...

We are exiles in this world, God's elect people, traveling toward our amazing inheritance—so we rejoice through trials, as they prove we have genuine faith.

Setting our hope on Christ changes our thinking and actions now, and shows itself by the way we sincerely love God's family in our church.

Talkabout

1. What is the most impressive building you've ever seen? How did it make you feel?

Investigate

📖 **Read 1 Peter 2:4-8**

DICTIONARY

Spiritual house (v 5): temple.
Priesthood (v5): priests represented the people to God, and God to the people.

Cornerstone (v 6): the first stone to be laid in a building, upon which the rest of the building rested and relied.

---

2. What is God building, and what with (v 5)?

"Spiritual house" is temple language. In the Old Testament, the temple was the place where God had promised to meet with his people; where the priests spoke to God about the people and to the people about God; and where the people could bring their animal sacrifices so that they could be forgiven and stay in relationship with God.

3. Those who "come to him" (v 4)—to the Lord Jesus, by faith—are the stones God uses to build his temple. So what is Peter saying about the church—Christians?

4. What are we told about the cornerstone of this divinely designed and divinely built building (v 4, 6-8)?

Apply

5. How do these verses excite you about being part of God's church?

- How should they affect your view of what you are doing as you "go to church" next Sunday?

6. "Christianity is offensive." True or false?

Getting Personal | OPTIONAL

The human heart loves to construct a platform upon which we will be made much of. Even if it's only in our own family or workplace or church, we want to be famous and praised. But the church exists to make much of Jesus. It is his fame we are to work for and his name we should want to be praised.

How has the description of the church in these verses motivated you to care less about your own fame and more about the Lord's? How will you work for his praise, even at the expense of yours, this week?

Investigate

📖 **Read 1 Peter 1:9-12**

DICTIONARY

Race (v 9): people.
Sojourners (v 11): temporary visitors.
Abstain (v 11): restrain yourself; refuse to be influenced by.
Flesh (v 11): our natural, sinful selves.

Gentiles (v 12): non-Christians.
Day of visitation (v 12): the day when Jesus returns in power and glory.

---

7. Read Exodus 19:5-6 and Isaiah 43:20-21. What is Peter telling us about the identity of the church in 1 Peter 2:9?

- Imagine you are one of Peter's first readers—marginalized and misunderstood by your society. How would verse 9 encourage you? What dangers would it guard you against?

8. What is one purpose of the church, according to verse 9? How do local churches do this?

Explore More | OPTIONAL

📖 Read Hosea 1 and 1 Peter 2:10

- How does Peter link what has happened to these believers in Asia Minor (and in your locality today) with what God prophesied through Hosea?
- How does God describe the natural state of his people ("land") in Hosea 1:2?
- So why is it astonishing that we should be treated as "children of God," who "have received mercy"?

---

9. What is a second purpose of the church (v 12)?

- What is the aim of doing this (end of verse 12)?

- How are these two purposes linked?

It is easy to think that our problems are "out there" in the Christ-rejecting world, and that we need to withdraw and insulate ourselves from the sinful world around us in order to remain holy.

10. How would that prevent us fulfilling our purpose as God's church?

- Why is that approach to pursuing holiness futile in any case (v 11)?

Apply

11. How is your own church both declaring and displaying the beauty of living under God's loving rule:
   - to one another?

   - to those around you?

- Are you in any way at risk of prioritizing one of these but ignoring the other?

12. Share what has particularly excited you during this study about being part of the church.

Getting Personal | OPTIONAL

What truth about the identity of your church are you going to remember and enjoy as you walk into your next church service? How will that shape your thoughts and actions during and after the service?

Pray

Thank God that Christ is the precious, tested cornerstone.

Thank God for your church. Use each of the descriptions in verses 9-12 to praise God for the privilege it is to be part of his church.

Pray that God would enable you to see how you are being called to declare and display his excellencies, individually and as a church.

Pray for particular non-Christians you know who are in touch with your church in some way—that what they see in you and hear from you would cause them to glorify God now and on the day when he returns.

4

In His Footsteps

1 Peter 2:13 – 3:7

The Story So Far...

We are exiles in this world, God's elect people, traveling toward our amazing inheritance—so we rejoice through trials, as they prove we have genuine faith.

Setting our hope on Christ changes our thinking and actions now, and shows itself by the way we sincerely love God's family in our church.

The church is God's magnificent building, founded on Christ, lived in by his Spirit, built out of people, and existing to declare and display his excellencies.

Talkabout

1. How do you respond to the word "submit"? Is submitting a positive thing or a negative thing?

Investigate

Peter is going to show us how to "keep [our] conduct among the Gentiles honorable, so that ... they may see your good deeds and glorify God on the day of visitation" (2:12). And his theme here is: "Be subject."

📖 **Read 1 Peter 2:13 – 3:7**

DICTIONARY

Be subject (2:13): submit.
Brotherhood (v 17): your church; other Christians.
Righteousness (v 24): the way God wants people to live.
Gentle (3:4): humble, not harsh.

Quiet (v 4): a calming presence that brings peace.
Weaker vessel (v 7): Peter simply means that, generally speaking, God created women as physically weaker than men.

---

2. Who are Christians to "be subject" to (2:13-14, 18; 3:1)?

   • How do you respond to these three "be subject" commands? Why?

3. How does Peter detail what it means to "be subject" in each of these areas?
   • 2:15-17

   • 2:18-19

   • 3:2, 4

Getting Personal |

In what ways do you find it hardest to submit to the authorities?

How does this passage both challenge and motivate you to do so?

How will you ensure that you remember this passage at the moment when you need to?

Explore More | OPTIONAL

When we serve governing authorities, we are, in fact, serving God. But there are exceptions to the command to "be subject to" all authorities. Peter himself showed this...

📖 **Read Acts 5:17-32**

- How do Peter's conduct and words here help us to understand when Christians are not to "be subject to" the authorities?
- Can you think of examples in your own society when you might need respectfully to tell an authority that you "must obey God rather than men"?

4. What motivations does Peter gives for submitting in these three ways?
   - 2:15

   - 2:20b

   - 3:1, 4b

5. What do you think it means for a husband to treat his wife "in an understanding way" (3:7)?

- Why would this make it easier for a wife gladly to "be subject to" him?

6. What is the sign that a husband is loving his wife well (v 7b)? Why is this, do you think?

Apply

7. How do each of these "be subject" commands look today, in your life?

- When is being subject in these ways hardest for you, and why? How has this passage encouraged and challenged you to submit nonetheless?

Investigate

📖 **Reread 1 Peter 2:21-25**

8. What kind of life are we all called to live as Christians (v 21)?

9. What example did Jesus leave for us (v 22-23)?

10. In his suffering, Jesus is always our example; but how is he also far more than our example (v 24-25)?

- How should verses 24-25 move us to follow Jesus' example, do you think?

Apply

11. What has Peter shown us about what it will look like to worship Christ?

- What else are we tempted to worship at moments of unjust suffering?

12. How has this passage affected your expectations of your life, and your view of suffering in your life?

Getting Personal | OPTIONAL

"Christ also suffered for you, leaving you an example, so that you might follow in his steps" (v 21).

We tend to be very pleased that Jesus bore his cross for us, but hope that we can avoid bearing a cross as we follow him. We need to realize that suffering is part of living faithfully for all of us, and not merely an add-on for super-keen believers.

How will you follow in his steps this week? What might stop you doing so? How do you need others to pray for you?

Pray

Thank God:

- *that Jesus suffered for you. Spend time praising Christ for how he responded to unjust suffering.*

- *that Jesus is an example to us.*

Ask God:

- *to help you to be subject in the ways he calls you to be, and to help you see how you are following in Jesus' footsteps.*

- *to enable you to see the goodness of the Christian life, even when it is countercultural and costly.*

5

Christ Also Suffered

1 Peter 3:8 – 4:6

The Story So Far...

We are God's elect, exiles in this world, traveling toward our inheritance—so we rejoice through trials and sincerely love our church family.

The church is God's magnificent building, founded on Christ, lived in by his Spirit, built out of people, and existing to declare and display his excellencies.

We are called to follow in Christ's footsteps by submitting to authority even if we suffer unjustly. As we do, others see the reality and beauty of our faith.

Talkabout

Imagine that a researcher who knows nothing about Christianity is given three months to observe your church and interview its members.

1. What do you think they would conclude that the Christian life was like, and what conduct would they think was most important to Christians?

- Now imagine we give the same researcher a month to read the New Testament. Do you think they would change their conclusions at all? If so, how?

Investigate

📖 **Read 1 Peter 3:8-17**

---

2. How should we live (v 8-12)?

- For each command, think of a practical way in which this is different than how we would naturally conduct ourselves.

3. "Obtain" (v 9) is better translated "inherit." Reread 1:3-5. What do we know awaits us, and how does this enable us to suffer and to bless?

4. Why do Christians need neither to fear nor be troubled by those who harm them (3:13-14)?

• What should they do instead (v 15-16)?

• Why?

Apply

5. How would your life, conduct, and words be different if you really did not fear anything because you knew that the worst that can happen cannot happen—that you cannot lose God's love for you?

Verses 14-15 show that fearing man more than Christ is often what stops us speaking to others about the "reason for the hope that is in [us]."

6. What do verses 15-16 teach us about how to share our faith faithfully and effectively?

• Which aspect do you find hardest, and why? What encouragement or help do you need?

Explore More | OPTIONAL

Respond to one (or more) of these statements in a way that gives a reason for the hope that you have (in other words, that talks about Jesus), and does so "with gentleness and respect."

- Christianity is irrelevant.
- Science has disproved the Bible.
- A good God would not allow suffering.
- It is arrogant to say that Christianity is the only right religion.
- The Bible's teaching on sexual morality is outdated and bigoted.

Getting Personal | OPTIONAL

Reflect on your answers to questions 5 and 6.

What needs to change? How will it change? And how will honoring Christ as Lord in your heart mean you make these changes willingly and joyfully, rather than grudgingly?

Investigate

📖 Read 1 Peter 3:18-22

This passage is very hard to understand. Remember that Peter's aim throughout his letter is to encourage us to persevere faithfully in unjust suffering—so it's likely that this is his aim here too. Bear that in mind as we work through it!

7. What event do these verses begin with, and what event do they end with (v 18, 22)?

8. What did Jesus' death achieve (v 18)? How does this encourage us to stay faithful when we suffer?

"Made alive in the spirit" (v 18) refers to Jesus' resurrection. Peter is using "spirit"/"spiritual" in the same way Paul does in 1 Corinthians 15:46. Our flesh is corruptible and perishable—but when Jesus was raised "in the spirit," he was raised to incorruptible, imperishable spiritual life—still in a physical body, but now an eternal body.

So for both Peter and Paul, "spirit/spiritual" is not the opposite of "physical." And the "spirits in prison" (1 Peter 3:19) are likely the angels who disobeyed God at the time of the flood, "in the days of Noah" (v 20). After his resurrection, then, Jesus proclaimed his victory over these fallen angels.

9. How does knowing what Jesus did after his resurrection (v 19) and where Jesus is now (v 22) encourage us to stay faithful when we suffer?

The complexities are not over yet! In verse 21, Peter says baptism is a picture of God's rescue from the floodwaters of his judgment and into new life, enjoying a "good conscience" (that is, Christ's perfect record)—just as Noah was rescued from the flood of God's judgment, into new life (v 20).

10. So, as we look back to our baptism, what are we meant to remember that we can look forward to?

- How does this encourage us to remain faithful when we suffer?

Here is a helpful summary of what Peter is teaching in these verses:

Why is it better to suffer for doing good (v 17)? Because Jesus has already walked the road marked with righteous suffering—and it was the pathway to his vindication and glory. Let your baptism remind you that you are on the same pathway.

📖 Read 1 Peter 4:1-6

11. How should we think and live (v 1-2)?

- Why will this make life harder, not easier (v 3-4)?

- What can we remember when living "for the will of God" is hard (v 5-6)?

Apply

12. Paul told some young Christians, "Through many tribulations we must enter the kingdom of God" (Acts 14:22). How is this verse a good summary of what Peter has taught us here?

Getting Personal | OPTIONAL

How has this passage helped you to appreciate your baptism?

How can you "use" your baptism next time you are tempted to avoid suffering for doing what is good?

Pray

Use 1 Peter 3:18 to praise the Lord Jesus for all he achieved for you through his suffering.

Use verse 22 to praise Jesus for his power and rule right now.

Share how you need God's help to give an answer for the hope you have in a respectful, gentle way; and pray for one another.

Share how you need God's help to live by his will, rather than according to "human passions"; and pray for one another.

6

Stand Firm, for the End Is at Hand

1 Peter 4:7 - 5:14

The Story So Far...

We are God's elect, exiles in this world, traveling joyfully through trials to our inheritance—part of his church, existing to declare and display his excellencies.

We are called to follow in Christ's footsteps by submitting to authority even if we suffer unjustly. As we do, others see the reality and beauty of our faith.

Christ's path went through suffering to vindication and inheritance; his people's path will be the same. On our way, we bless others and live by God's will.

Talkabout

1. If you knew the world would end in 24 hours, how would you spend your last day? Who with? And how would you feel?

Investigate

📖 **Read 1 Peter 4:7-11**

2. What does Peter remind us of (v 7)?

• Read 1:3-4, 7. How do you feel about knowing this day is "at hand"?

3. What implications will knowing that this day is coming have (4:7-11)?

Getting Personal | OPTIONAL

What would practicing hospitality without grumbling look like for you in your circumstances and culture?

How are you using, or how could you starting using, the gifts God has given you to serve others in the church?

📖 **Read 1 Peter 4:12-19**

As we have seen repeatedly through this letter, between the day we put our faith in Christ and the day Christ returns at "the end of all things," we will suffer because we follow him.

4. In the face of this "fiery trial," what should we not be (v 12)?

- What should we do, and why (v 13-16, 19)?

Explore More | OPTIONAL

- What has already begun "at the household of God"—the church (v 17)?

📖 **Read Matthew 25:31-46**

- Who is being separated from whom here, and when?
- How does suffering in this life separate those two groups within the visible church?
- How does this help us understand what Peter means in 1 Peter 4:17?

Apply

5. How has the whole of 1 Peter helped you to be neither surprised about nor despairing at the reality that the Christian life is a life of suffering?

• How has it helped you to respond to that suffering with joy?

Investigate

The end is near, but the time between now and then will be hard. What if we lose our heads and wander away from Christ like straying sheep? What if we face situations where we simply do not know what to do?

📖 **Read 1 Peter 5:1-5**

DICTIONARY

Exhort (v 1): strongly encourage; urge.
Elders (v 1): church leaders.

Partaker (v 1): sharer.
Domineering (v 3): controlling in a dominating, aggressive way.

---

6. Who has God given to his church to help Jesus' "sheep" (v 1-2a)?

7. What should elders do, and remember (v 2-4)?

- What should church members do, and remember (v 5)?

Getting Personal | OPTIONAL

It is as the shepherds lead and the sheep follow that we all walk confidently and hopefully toward the end of all things and the inheritance that is ours. If we have elders who are "followable"—who are the kind of men Peter describes here—we need to be humble and follow them!

Are there any ways in which you have had to be humble and follow your elders, or follow them without grumbling about it?

Do you pray for your elders, and for your own humble following? How can you make sure you do so regularly?

And if you are an elder, do you pray for your sheep, and for your own humble leadership?

📖 Read 1 Peter 5:6-14

Exalt (v 6): lift up.

Babylon (v 13): Peter likely means Rome.

---

8. What should our attitude be toward…
   - God?

   - the devil?

- our suffering?

At the end of verse 12, Peter lays out his purpose in writing this letter. He wants to remind these suffering Christians of "the true grace of God." Why? So that they would "stand firm in it."

9. Flick your eyes over the letter. How would it have encouraged the Christians to "stand firm"?

- How would it have showed them what it looks like each day to "stand firm"?

Apply

10. Share how the letter has encouraged you to "stand firm" as a Christian.

- Share one or two things that the Spirit has been prompting you to change in your thoughts or actions as you have studied 1 Peter.

11. This guide is titled *Living Well on the Way Home*. Use this letter to sum up in one sentence each…
   - what is exciting about our future home.

   - how we can live well, in God's sight, on our way there.

Pray

Choose a verse from 1 Peter that moves you to praise God, and use it to worship him together now.

Share your greatest challenge from the book, and pray for one another.

Finish by thanking God that the end of all things is at hand, and that because of Jesus' suffering and resurrection, you are able to look forward to that day as the day that you will enter your inheritance.

1 Peter

*Living Well on the
Way Home*

LEADER'S
GUIDE

Leader's Guide: Introduction

This Leader's Guide includes guidance for every question. It will provide background information and help you if you get stuck. For each session, you'll also find the following:

The Big Idea: The main point of the session, in brief. This is what you should be aiming to have fixed in people's minds by the end of the session!

Summary: An overview of the passage you're reading together.

Optional Extra: Usually this is an introductory activity that ties in with the main theme of the Bible study and is designed to break the ice at the beginning of a session. Or it may be a "homework project" that people can tackle during the week.

Occasionally the Leader's Guide includes an extra follow-up question, printed in *italics*. This doesn't appear in the main study guide but could be a useful add-on to help your group get to the answer or go deeper.

Here are a few key principles to bear in mind as you prepare to lead:

- Don't just read out the answers from the Leader's Guide. Ideally, you want the group to discover these answers from the Bible for themselves.

- Keep drawing people back to the passage you're studying. People may come up with answers based on their experiences or on teaching they've heard in the past, but the point of this study is to listen to God's word itself—so keep directing your group to look at the text.

- Make sure everyone finishes the session knowing how the passage is relevant for them. We do Bible study so that our lives can be changed by what we hear from God's word. So, **Apply** questions aren't just an add-on—they're a vital part of the session.

Finally, remember that your group is unique! You should feel free to use this Good Book Guide in a way that works for them. If they're a quiet bunch, you might want to spend longer on the **Talkabout** question. If they love to get creative, try using mind-mapping or doodling to kick-start some of your discussions. If your time is limited, you can choose to skip **Explore More** or split the whole session into two. Adapt the material in whatever way you think will help your group get the most out of God's word.

1

Certain Future, Joyful Present

1 Peter 1:1-12

The Big Idea

Christians are God's chosen people, exiles in the world as we walk to the inheritance he has prepared for us and is leading us to—so hardships and suffering are not disasters, but opportunities joyfully to see the genuineness of our faith.

Summary

In our own day it is becoming increasingly difficult to live as a Christian. It feels more and more that we're exiles in a world we once called our own. Our culture seems to misunderstand us more and more, and to malign and mock us more and more.

Peter wants to show us that this is not strange. Those who desire to live godly lives in this world will be persecuted. Christian suffering is normal.

And Peter wants us to keep going through the suffering. In this first study, you will see first that our identity is one of "elect exiles" (1:1)—exiles because we do not belong in this world, and elect because we are chosen by God to trust in Christ, through his Spirit, to be his people (v 2). Since God chose us before the creation of the world, he is hardly going to let us go now!

Second, Peter will point us toward our inheritance, which never fades, never becomes defiled, and never perishes, and which God is going to bring us to (v 3-5). It is some inheritance—and it inspires in

us a future hope that allows us to endure whatever we face in this life.

Third, Peter tells us that the trials we face show us the genuineness of our faith (v 6-7). When we are tested but keep trusting, we can look at our faith and know it is real; and we can look forward to hearing God's approval and praise when Jesus Christ returns. So we can rejoice even as we suffer.

Fourth, Peter points out that though life may be very hard, we are in a privileged position. The prophets would have loved to live in a time such as ours (v 10-12), after the cross and resurrection; and the angels would love to experience a salvation such as ours: rescue by Jesus (v 12).

All this should enable us to live joyfully in our present because we know our future is secure and wonderful—and therefore to praise God for all he has done, is doing, and will do for us (v 3)!

Optional Extra

Visit a local travel agent and pick up a few brochures showcasing a variety of vacations (lake, city break, snow, etc.). Alternatively, find some vacation websites to show to your group. Ask your group members to use the brochures/websites to come up with their ideal vacation break. Then ask them how knowing they were heading off on that vacation in six months' time would make them feel…

- when they had a good day.
- when they had a bad day.
- when they were tired, or disappointed.

The point is that what is coming in our future makes a difference to how we feel (and act) in the present. You could return to this after question 4, 6, or 7.

Guidance for Questions

1. **What do you expect the Christian life to be like between here and heaven?**

   Allow all kinds of answers. (There is no "wrong answer" at this point.) Some may have a more optimistic view—others more pessimistic; some may never have really thought about it.

- **What makes you answer like that?**

   This question encourages your group to think about the source/authority of their view of how life will be. It might be past experience; the media; their church; or the Bible. Encourage them as you go through this study (and the whole book of 1 Peter) to compare and contrast their answer with Peter's answer. You could return to this question at the end of your study.

2. **How does the apostle Peter describe the Christians in what is now modern-day Turkey whom he is writing to (v 1)?**
   - *Elect*—that is, God's chosen people, related to God because of his divine choice.
   - *Exiles*—Peter is using Old Testament imagery, of Israel (God's people), who were exiled to

Babylon. We are foreigners in this world: we do not belong; we are just passing through.

- **What does this tell us about how Peter wants us to view our relationship with God?**

   We belong to God because he has chosen to love us. Nothing—no amount of hardship or difficulty or our own failings—can change this.

- **What does it tell us about how Peter wants us to view our life in this world?**

   It will be the life of exiles. We will be treated as strange and different—even hated (see John 15:18-19). We are just passing through—sojourners (1 Peter 2:11). We will never, and should never, "belong" here or feel "at home" here.

3. **What have the three Persons of the Trinity done for each Christian (v 2)? Put each phrase into your own words.**
   - God the Father chose people "according to [his] foreknowledge." Foreknowledge does not just mean that the Father foresaw who would respond to his offer of salvation; it means he had planned to save his people before the creation of the world (in the same way as he planned to send his Son, v 20).
   - The Spirit sanctified us "for obedience to Jesus Christ." "Sanctification" means "set apart for," or "dedicated to." So here, Peter uses the word to mean that the Spirit sets

apart those the Father has chosen "for obedience" to the gospel—to repent of their sin and trust in Christ.

- We are able to repent and trust because of Jesus' blood, with which we are sprinkled. This is a strange phrase, but it refers back to how God told Moses to take the blood of an animal that had been sacrificed in place of the people of Old Testament Israel, and throw it over the people as a sign that, as God's covenant people, they were forgiven through that sacrificial offering (Exodus 24:8).

4. **What has "the God and Father of our Lord Jesus Christ" done for his people (v 3-4)?**

- He has caused us to be "born again"—we are now children of God, with a new life and new identity.
- This means that we have "a living hope." "Hope" in the Bible is not a vague wish, but a certain expectation of a future event. This hope is grounded in "the resurrection of Jesus Christ from the dead," which proves to us that we, like him, will enjoy life beyond death, and that this hard life of trials and suffering is not all there is. We will follow Christ through death and into life.
- Not only will we enjoy a future resurrection, but we will live in our future inheritance. Just as Israel's scattered exiles were promised that they would return to God's promised land, so we have an inheritance

to look forward to. But unlike that of Israel, our inheritance is "imperishable, undefiled, and unfading." It is eternal, pure, and perfect. Encourage your group to appreciate just how wonderful life in this inheritance will be, and how different than life now, where even the best moments are flawed, or cannot last.

5. **How could Peter's first readers— and we—know they would reach this inheritance (v 5)? Why is this encouraging?**

Because the God who keeps our inheritance secure in heaven (v 4) also keeps his children going in faith until they reach it (v 5). God's power shields us through this life—not from suffering, but from unbelief. This is very encouraging, because (as we'll see) we will face suffering, persecution, and temptation. If we had to get ourselves to our promised inheritance—if our faith were up to us—then we should worry that we might lose our faith in hard times. So it is wonderful and reassuring to know that we will reach heaven, not because of our strength but because of God's power—he not only gave us saving faith, but he will sustain and strengthen our faith through all that comes our way.

6. **How do these verses encourage us to live for what we will have in the future, rather than what we could have in our present?**

By telling us to identify ourselves as exiles—we are not to expect or demand or even desire a comfortable, or wealthy, or trouble-free, or popular life now. If we remember that we are exiles, passing through, we won't be surprised or despair when troubles come or we have less than those around us in worldly terms.

Equally, Peter points us forwards to our future—it is a future worth living for (and dying for)! Our future is unimaginably better than anything this world can offer—it will make the most exotic places and the finest moments of our lives pale in comparison. This inspires in us a future-looking hope that allows us to endure even the most oppressive circumstances on earth.

7. In what areas of life would thinking of yourselves as "elect exiles" change the way you think, feel, or act?
This will vary according to your context and each individual's circumstances. Allow your group time to think and talk about ways they may be forgetting that they are exiles, passing through, who don't belong; or ways they may not be living with their relationship to God and their future inheritance in mind.

8. How is it possible—and right—for Christians to rejoice in trials (v 6-9)?
In verse 6, Peter is continuing his thought from verses 3-5—we rejoice (literally, we are exceedingly joyful) because we know we are chosen by God, kept by God's power, and heading for our wonderful inheritance. No trial can change any of that. Whatever happens, we know we are walking toward the day when Christ is revealed and we receive the "outcome of [our] faith, the salvation of [our] souls" (v 9).

Because our joy is rooted in God and his salvation, it does not fluctuate—it does not rise and fall according to our present circumstances. If our joy is found from knowing whose we are, and where we are heading, then our joy will always be great.

Further, in verse 7 Peter explains that Christian suffering is a fire through which our faith is both refined and proven to be genuine. As gold is put through fire to remove its impurities, so are believers. As we faithfully endure through a hard time, we prove to ourselves and to others that our faith is real, and we can look forward to such faith being rewarded (with salvation) when Christ is revealed (v 7).

NOTE: Peter is not calling us to rejoice about suffering itself—we can rejoice in and despite suffering, but we're not to seek to masochistically rejoice about the suffering.

9. How is this different than how the world links trials and joy?
Because a trial involves the removal of something that the world says we need in order to be fulfilled and satisfied and joyful (or else it would not be a trial), the world says that trials and suffering will diminish or destroy our joy. So, when facing a

trial, the world tells us that we need to avoid it, try to ignore it, or just get through it as quickly as we can so that we might be joyful again. But Christians are different: we can be joyful in a trial, because our joy rests on knowing God and being saved by him, and the trial cannot remove these things; and because in that trial we can see that our faith, as we continue to trust Christ, is truly genuine—it endures in the hard times—and this brings us joy too.

10. **How are believers who live after Christ's death and resurrection in a privileged position compared to...**

- **the Old Testament prophets (v 10-12)?**
Because the prophets predicted and pointed toward the coming of the Messiah, his suffering, and his glory—but they did not know when or how he would achieve this (v 11). But Peter's readers know the time and circumstances of the Messiah's life, death, and resurrection, because they live after it. They can enjoy knowing exactly when and how Jesus has come and saved them—something the prophets never could have done. Isaiah, Elijah, and the other prophets would gladly have time-traveled to our day, to live as a Christian in our time!

- **the angels in heaven (v 12)?**
Angels live in the throne room of heaven; they have observed the unfolding of God's salvation plan; they rejoice when a sinner repents (Luke 15:10); but they will never

experience God's salvation, because it is only humans whom God saves. In this sense, they "long to look" into these things—they do not know what it is like to experience the relief, the joy, the liberation, and the wonder of being a saved sinner. We do!

Explore More

○ **What did the Spirit do in Old Testament times (v 11)?**
He revealed to the prophets the future suffering and glories of the Christ. The prophets were not speaking on their own authority, proclaiming their own guesswork; they were speaking what God's Spirit had revealed to them, on his authority (see 2 Peter 1:21).

○ **Read Isaiah 52:13 – 53:12. How does this prophecy point forwards to "the sufferings of Christ and the subsequent glories"?**
His sufferings: 52:14; 53:1-9. His glories: 52:13, 1; 53:10-12.

○ **Why is it a privilege to read it now, after Christ's death, resurrection, and ascension, rather than to hear it as Isaiah's first listeners did?**
Because we are able to know how God's suffering servant, his Christ, fulfilled Isaiah's words, so we can appreciate and enjoy what the Spirit revealed to the prophet all the more.

○ **What else has the Spirit done (1 Peter 1:12)?**
Caused people to preach "the good

news to you." The Spirit who spoke through the prophets to predict the saving work of Christ now speaks through his people to proclaim the saving work of Christ.

○ **Briefly share how he did this for you.**

With the emphasis on "briefly," share your stories of how the Spirit caused the gospel to come to you through the words of others, and enabled you to put your faith in Christ.

---

11. **What stops us from greatly rejoicing during "various trials"?**

Put simply, it is having a worldly view of trials rather than a Christian one (see question 9). So we react to hardships with surprise, or anger, or hopelessness, or despair, or by trying to ignore them or gritting our teeth to get through them. We need to read and believe and meditate on verses 3-9!

• **How can we unwittingly discourage fellow Christians from rejoicing when they suffer?**

By responding and speaking in worldly ways, rather than in gospel-focused ways. If we speak to our brothers and sisters about their suffering without mentioning the gospel, or without reminding them that there are good reasons to be joyful in and despite their trials, then we are actually encouraging them to respond "naturally" to their trial—i.e. without joy.

• **How can we consciously encourage each other to rejoice in these times?**

Think about how you might speak of verses 3-9 in a way that does not sound insensitive or glib, and of practical things you can do; and remember that we need to pray for each other in these circumstances (for joy in the trial, rather than merely an end to the trial). You could come up with a scenario to discuss (e.g. a member of your group is bullied at work for their faith; or loses a friendship when they share their faith; or struggles with a long-term, chronic illness)—or, if a member of your group is facing a hard trial at the moment, you could ask them beforehand to share what would be helpful for them (and what they find unhelpful) in order to encourage them to be joyful.

2

Loving Christ by Loving Your Church

1 Peter 1:13 - 2:3

The Big Idea

As Christians, we set our hope on our future with Christ, which changes our thinking and actions now; and we enjoy being part of God's family, which shows itself in how we love our church.

Summary

Peter has sought to encourage his readers by grounding them in the glorious salvation planned, accomplished, and applied by the triune God on their behalf (v 1-9). He has reminded them that they live in a time of fulfillment, when they are privileged to experience what the prophets looked forward to and what the angels wondered over (v 10-12).

But the question remains: What are they to do? How are they to go about relating to this hostile world? How are they to relate to one another in the midst of such difficult circumstances? These are the questions that we are grappling with today, and which Peter now addresses. From 1:13 – 2:3, Peter exhorts his readers regarding…

- where they are to set their hope (1:13): not on the things of this world, but on the grace God has given us through Christ.
- how they are to think and act differently as a result (v 14-16): alert and

sober thinking leads to obedience and holiness—which will mean we are very different than how we were before we came to faith.

- how they are to relate to God (v 17-21) and how they are to relate to one another as Christians (v 22-25): Peter shows that truly hoping in Christ and desiring to be holy like God will be seen in how we love others in our church. If we are God's elect, we are born into a new family—his family—and we are to love other Christians in a sincere, unhypocritical way.
- what they are to crave if they are to grow into the salvation that Peter has already described (2:1-3): deeper knowledge of and relationship wit, the Lord, who has saved us through his word.

Optional Extra

Ask group members to bring photographs of two of their grandparents or their parents with them, and give them to you as they arrive. Arrange them randomly on a table, and ask group members to write down which photos they think belong to which other member. Probably, some will be easy, due to shared physical characteristics in that family. (If you have people in your group who are adopted, ask them to talk about non-physical characteristics that they have picked up from their adoptive family. It might be better to start here, and not look at the photographs if this has the potential to be upsetting.) Move into a discussion about shared non-physical characteristics, and then on into the study, picking up on this activity after question 8, 10, or 11. We share non-physical characteristics in God's family; in this study, Peter identifies its eternal nature and its love.

Guidance for Questions

1. **"I love Jesus, but not the church." Have you ever heard anyone say something like that (or thought it yourself)?**

- **Why do people have this opinion?** They might...
  - allege that the church has become an unrecognizable institution influenced more by worldly practices than the New Testament.
  - feel that the church is filled with hypocrites who are even worse than those who deny Christ.
  - have themselves been hurt, or worse, by a church member or congregation.

- **Do you think it's justified? Why?** In this study, we'll see that while many of these critiques ring true, they're not legitimate reasons for Christians to give up on the church. But here, allow people to discuss when and how there might be justification for this view, and then you can return

to discuss the issue when you reach question 12.

2. **Where is the Christian's hope to be (v 13)?** "On the grace that will be brought to you at the revelation of Jesus Christ." Refer your group back to verse 4— the "grace" is the undeserved inheritance that is ours through faith in Christ because God has already worked through Christ to secure our future. Make sure your group understands that this is not a false or uncertain wish ("I hope my team wins the championship this year") but a certainty about a future event.

3. **How will setting our hopes here change our thinking and our actions (v 13-16)?**

- Our minds will be "[prepared] for action" and "sober" (v 13). "Preparing your minds for action" is literally "girding up the loins of your minds"—a picture of a man preparing to exercise by gathering his robe and tucking it into his belt. So the idea is that we need minds that are ready to be disciplined, to work at focusing on our future hope. This is why we need to be "sober-minded"—to think clearly about reality. To set our hope on God and our future salvation, we need to not be "drunk" on the priorities and promises of this world, but clear-sighted about who God is and all he gives. This will require mental effort.
- We will be "obedient" (v 14).

Negatively, this means we won't live as we did before we knew God and the future that now will be ours. We won't follow evil desires. Positively, we'll seek to be like God—"holy"—in all that we do (v 15-16). How we live in this world reveals to whom we are dedicated—to the world or to God?

4. How does Peter motivate us to live in this way?

* **v 17**

  By reminding us that God judges. One day, we will have to give an account for everything we have done, thought, and said (see Matthew 12:33-37). Our deeds matter: we will one day explain our conduct to the one who can throw people into hell, and that ought to make us live with "fear" (1 Peter 1:17). When we are tempted to live in an unholy way, we can motivate ourselves to be holy instead by remembering who God is, how powerful he is, and saying to ourselves, "One day I will have to account for the way the next ten minutes of my life are spent."

* **v 18-21**

  Primarily, though, we are to conduct ourselves with gratitude. Peter reminds us of the cost of our redemption by using the theme of Israel's redemption from slavery in Egypt (see Exodus 12). We have been freed ("ransomed," 1 Peter 1:18) from the emptiness of life without God and with no future—which cost the "precious blood of Christ" (v 19), the

perfect Lamb. This was always God's plan (v 20)—it was no divine after-thought. This is why the Judge is our Father (v 17)—and Peter is telling us to consider the cost of our redemption, and the love of God in planning that redemption, and that this will motivate us to pursue holiness out of gratitude.

5. Choose one or more of the following problems that we may identify as being the biggest problem in our lives: poverty, singleness, illness, boredom. Then identify…

* **what that might cause us to locate our hope in.**
  * *Poverty*: You may set your hope in education, or crime, as a way out.
  * *Singleness*: You may set your hope in finding a good man or a loving woman.
  * *Illness*: You may set your hope in modern medicine, or Eastern meditation, or a particular doctor.
  * *Boredom*: You may set your hope in experiences.

* **how that would influence our thinking and actions.**
  Where your hope is, you think most about and you focus most on. It is your priority—and so that drives your actions. I might break the law in order to gain wealth; or I might marry someone unwisely, because then I won't be lonely; or I'll spend all my savings pursuing an unlikely cure for an illness; and so on. Equally, if my hopes are dashed, then my thinking will become negative and

despairing, and that again will impact my actions. The aim of these questions is to help the group see that where we place our hope is what directs both our thoughts and actions, for better or for worse.

- **How do verses 17-19 help us to have our "hope ... in God" (v 21)?**
  Think about what our biggest problem truly is. It is facing God in judgment without being saved (v 17); it is living our lives in emptiness, without purpose or future (v 18). So our only hope is in God working to save us from his judgment and free us from this empty way of life—and that is exactly what he has done, at great cost, through Christ's death (v 18-19). So knowing our greatest problem, and knowing who has saved us from that and how, will mean that we truly do place all our hope in God, knowing that he has redeemed us and will give us our inheritance.

6. **Why is it liberating to set our hope on Jesus' return?**
   This question refers back to something we looked at in the last study—that our hope (and joy) is based on something separate from our current circumstances, so it is solid and not fluctuating. Jesus' return is certain, and his death and resurrection mean we can look forward to it with hope as God's children, rather than with fear as unredeemed sinners. So our hope is in something that is wonderful, that is certain, and that cannot be taken away. Everyone hopes in something; and having our hope in God and on Jesus' return is the only hope that will "deliver" eternally.

- **Why is it hard to keep our hope there?**
  Because the rest of the world does not. We are surrounded by people encouraging us to place our hope in present wealth, or health, or relationships, or experiences, and so on. It is hard to keep a future focus, and to set our hopes on someone that we cannot see and something that has not yet happened—which is why we need to make the effort in our minds (v 13).

7. **How does Peter compare and contrast the way we are brought into a natural family and the way we are brought into God's family (1:23-25)?**
   - We are brought into our natural family through procreation ("seed," v 23), but into God's family through the "living and abiding word of God"—i.e. by obeying the gospel call to repent and believe.
   - Every human family is "perishable" (i.e. no human family lasts for ever, since those who are born into it will certainly die and leave it); being "born again" into God's people means we are "imperishable"— this is a family that lasts forever. Peter reinforces these points by quoting in verses 24-25 from Isaiah 40:6-8—humans are like grass, which withers (so those who are

born to humans will do likewise), but the word of God endures forever, and so those who are born into God's family through that word will also endure forever.

8. What is the great "family characteristic" we are to grow in (v 22)?

"Sincere brotherly love": notice the familial wording—a love that is "from a pure heart."

- **Read 1 John 4:7-11. How does our Father both show us and motivate us to grow in our family likeness?**

We know what love is because God has shown it to us, by sending his Son to die for us. We love, not to earn God's love but because he has already loved us. And if we truly do know God's love, then we will love others—if God has poured his astonishing, gracious love into us, then it will overflow as love for others.

9. What has no place in God's imperishable family (1 Peter 2:1)?

- "Malice": a general word for evil that carries with it hostility and possibly even an intention to cause harm.
- "Deceit": concealing the truth to cause someone to believe something that isn't true, usually for our own ends.
- "Hypocrisy": putting on a mask so that people think better of us than they would if the truth were known.
- "Envy": rooted in covetousness, this is holding ill will toward someone because they have an apparent advantage over us.
- "Slander": speaking evil of someone to bring them harm.

Point out to your group that all these words represent sins of both general and specific evil against people. They are all sins that harm relationships and destroy community. In other words, they all work against the command to "love one another earnestly" (1:22). If I am to love my Christian brothers and sisters, I must also be ridding myself of these sins.

10. How do we grow as members of this family (v 2-3)?

By craving "pure spiritual milk" (v 2). To "crave" means to desire with great intensity—we are to crave pure spiritual milk as a newborn baby craves its mother's milk. And this "milk" is the same word through which we are born again. Peter is saying that we will grow as Christians—grow in love and rid ourselves of sin—as we take in the word of God, by reading Scripture on our own and together. And we motivate ourselves to do this by remembering that we have "tasted that the Lord is good" (v 3). We have experienced that the Lord is good—he has saved us!—so we want to experience more of his goodness by "drinking in" his word. We know God by his word, and we grow more like God through his word. We get a taste for it.

Explore More

○ **Read Romans 12:9-21. What kind of love does Paul tell us to have (v 9)?**
"Genuine." Just as Peter wants us to think about what "sincere" love is, so Paul encourages us to make sure that our love is "genuine."

○ **What does this look like in practice: in how we treat other believers and in how we treat those around us?**
For each of these means of loving others genuinely, encourage your group to identify specifically and practically what that would look like in their own lives:
- Abhor what is evil; hold fast to what is good (v 9).
- Love "with brotherly affection ... showing honor" (v 10).
- Don't be "slothful in zeal," but "be fervent in spirit [and] serve the Lord" (v 11).
- Rejoice in hope (v 12).
- Be patient in tribulation (v 12).
- Be constant in prayer (v 12).
- Contribute to others' needs (v 13).
- Show hospitality (v 13).
- Bless, rather than cursing, those who persecute you (v 14).
- "Rejoice with those who rejoice, weep with those who weep" (v 15).
- "Live in harmony" by neither being haughty or not associating with "the lowly" (v 16).
- Repay no one with evil for evil, but live publicly in a way that is "honorable" so that you can live "peaceably" (v 17-18).
- Don't seek revenge, but seek to bless those who wrong you, so that you can "overcome evil with good" (v 19-21).

---

11. **What does "sincere brotherly love" for one another look like in practice for your church? Would a newcomer to your church describe your relationships in this way? Why / why not?**
This is an opportunity to think practically (both positively and negatively) about your own church. Probably, it is sincerely loving in many ways; probably it is not perfectly loving in every way. Think about how you spend your time, and what you do and speak about when you are together, both formally and informally.

12. **"I love Jesus, but not the church." How would you use 1 Peter 1:22 – 2:3 to show someone that if we really love Jesus, then we will really love his church?**
When we were born again, we were born into a family that is characterized by gracious love. Our Father is love. In love, Jesus, our elder Brother, died in our place so that we may live. Love is in our DNA, and Jesus teaches us both what it looks like to treasure God above all, and so love him as is fitting, and what it looks like to love the church. Because we have been born anew through the living and abiding word of God, and because we have set ourselves apart from this world of hate when we obeyed the

gospel, we must, can, and will love one another. Since Jesus loved the church, so also will we, even when that is hard or seems impossible. And so we do not walk away from our brother and sisters—we walk toward them in sincere love, as God did to us in Christ. If I really do love Christ, then I will love the church that he loves so much, imperfect though that church is.

3

The Greatest Building

1 Peter 2:4-12

The Big Idea

The church is God's magnificent building, founded on Christ, lived in by his Spirit, and built out of people. It exists to declare and display Christ. We will be excited about being part of this building project!

Summary

This study should excite you and your group about being part of your church! Peter is teaching us about what the church is—and, therefore, why it is a wonderful privilege to be a part of it.

First, in verses 4-8, Peter uses the image of the temple. The temple was the place where God had promised to meet with his people. There, the priests represented God to the people and the people to God, and together, priests and people represented God's rule to the world. There, repentant Israelites would bring their sacrifices and find atonement for their sin.

Now, Peter says, the temple is… the church, made out of living stones—Christians—built on the cornerstone that people rejected but God has chosen and tested and announced as precious—the Lord Jesus.

Then, in verses 9-12, Peter uses descriptions of Old Testament Israel, but applies them to the church. Christians are a chosen race, a royal priesthood, and a holy nation. And so this identity sets the mission of the church—to declare the excellencies of Christ, and to display them in how we live.

All this means that we are a part of something much larger than ourselves.

No matter where we are, no matter how small our gathering, we are God's building project: God's temple. Wherever there is a true church, there the rule of God is displayed and the worth of Christ—the fame of Christ—is proclaimed. We need to have a far grander view of what our church is, and what our church does!

Optional Extra

Gather pictures of ten or twelve of the world's most impressive buildings, from a range of historical eras and geographical locations. Choose an unremarkable part of each (e.g. a step outside the White House, a bolt from the Eiffel Tower in Paris, France, or a window on the Empire State Building); print just that part of the building, and ask your group to identify the building. Then go back through, showing pictures of the whole building.

Open up a discussion about how impressive buildings are made up from countless, not particularly impressive parts—and that it is only when a large part of the building can be seen that it is impressive, and when the whole building can be seen that it is most spectacular. This is like the church—we often only see our tiny part of it, but (as we'll see in this study) each tiny part is amazing, because of the whole that it is a part of.

Guidance for Questions

1. **What is the most impressive building you've ever seen? How did it make you feel?**

   Impressive buildings often make us feel inspired, or small, or awed. You might like to ask this follow-up question: *How would you have felt if you'd been part of the construction of the building?* Once your group have seen how Peter describes church, you could return to this question (e.g. after question 4 or 5). The most impressive building we have ever seen is Christ's church,

and it should make us feel all these things!

o *OPTIONAL: If you had to describe your church in 12 words, what would you say?*
   You could ask your group to write down their answers on a piece of paper each—then write down Peter's description in verse 9 (a chosen race, a royal priesthood, a holy nation, God's special possession) on a large piece of paper, and after question 7, compare your answers with Peter's.

2. **What is God building, and what with (v 5)?**

   "A spiritual house," built out of "living stones."

3. **Those who "come to him" (v 4)— to the Lord Jesus, by faith—are the stones God uses to build his temple. So what is Peter saying about the church—Christians?**

   That things mentioned in verse 5 are now true of the church—and of your local church. The church is God's temple, where his Spirit dwells— where God meets with his people. It is where we gather to hear God speak to us, and where we celebrate Christ's once-for-all sacrifice as our Lamb, and commit to living as sacrifices in our lives. We are living stones made to be built into a living building. Every Christian is brought into God's building project, is built on the cornerstone, Christ, and shares in his identity and status.

4. What are we told about the cornerstone of this divinely designed and divinely built building (v 4, 6-8)?

○ *OPTIONAL: (If your group needs assistance to reach the answers below): How do people naturally view Jesus? How does God view Jesus?*

In these verses, Peter points to two views of Jesus. One is humanity's:

• Jesus was rejected by humans (v 4).

• People seek to "build" their lives, societies and religions without Jesus—they reject him as the cornerstone (v 7).

• Jesus causes people to "stumble" and is a rock of offense" (v 8)—that is, Jesus offends people because he does not fit in with how they want the world to be and how they like to view themselves.

The other view is God's:

• Jesus is chosen by God, and precious to him (v 4).

• Jesus is the "cornerstone" God had promised to lay as the foundation of his people (v 6—see Isaiah 28:16).

• Jesus is the one who will never let down or disappoint those who trust him (v 6).

5. How do these verses excite you about being part of God's church?

This question aims to underline what you have likely already seen in the previous questions, but it is easy to forget just how special the church is. It is a "building" constructed by God, to last eternally, where he dwells in his people by his Spirit. No one who is built on Jesus will ever regret it, or be "put to shame." All human building projects will one day crumble, but God's building project—the church—will last eternally.

• **How should they affect your view of what you are doing as you "go to church" next Sunday?**

In many ways! Let your group discuss how they have been individually struck by these great truths. Here are three suggestions:

• As we gather together, God is there with us. We don't have to conjure up his presence or beg him to show up. When we gather, he is with us because he is in us—we are his living stones.

• We are part of something much larger than ourselves. No matter how large or small our gathering, we are God's building project, and he will continue building it, and finish the work. Your church is a tiny part of a small section of a wall of the temple that God is building up throughout his world.

• Christianity is not an individual endeavor; we were created for community. Gathering as church is where we will most learn of God and be moved to praise him; where we are able to serve him as we serve each other; and where we will be equipped to live for him in our lives.

Take time to discuss further how we might feel about "going to church"—and what your group needs to pray about regarding their attitude toward church.

6. "Christianity is offensive." True or false?

Both! To everyone who hears and understands the truth about Jesus, he will be either the most wonderful news or the most offensive. This is because he demands total allegiance, and that our lives be centered on him, under his authority. He is not willing to be just one brick in our own building—he calls us to be built into his, in order for us not to face judgment and shame, but instead to be saved eternally.

We need to understand that Jesus is seen as offensive! And because he's seen that way, we need to be prepared to be rejected. It doesn't matter how kind or gracious we are; it doesn't matter how winsome or charming we are. This does not give us the license to be obnoxious, rude, or arrogant. Our behavior should never offend; but the truth about Jesus often will. So, let's be respectful and winsome, but let's also realize that as long as we embrace the Jesus of the Bible and everything he has commanded, people will be offended. If no one is ever offended by our Jesus, then we need to ask ourselves: which Jesus do we have?

○ *OPTIONAL: (To help your group think about the implications of the perceived offensiveness of Jesus for their life and witness): Since Jesus is seen as offensive, what should we expect will be the response to us as we live for Christ and particularly as we speak of him?*

7. Read Exodus 19:5-6 and Isaiah 43:20-21. What is Peter telling us about the identity of the church in 1 Peter 2:9?

You will need to help your group understand the meaning of the descriptions so that you can all begin to be excited by them!

- *A chosen race.* The church is a new race, made up of many ethnicities, chosen by God on the basis of his predetermined love (1 Peter 1:2) and born again of imperishable seed (v 23). The church is not accidental or coincidental—it is the product of God's plan to call a people to himself, through faith in his Son.

- *A royal priesthood.* "Priesthood" tells us that we have access to God's presence; that we represent God to the world by telling people about him; and that we offer sacrifices to God—not a sacrifice that forgives us (Jesus has already done that), but "thanks-offerings" (see Leviticus 7), in response to what he has done for us. (If you have time, you could turn to Romans 12:1.) "Royal" means we serve as priests in the King's presence, and that the church serves a ruling function in the kingdom of God (see Revelation 20:6).

- *A holy nation.* We are a distinctive nation, different from the world. The church reflects the character of its King—it is holy. But Israel was also to display God's rule to the surrounding nations—and the church is to do so too, today, living as part of the heavenly kingdom that has been revealed to the world wherever God's people are. (This theme is developed further in question 8.)

- *God's special possession.* This likely picks up on Isaiah 43:21 (God formed his people "for myself"). The church belongs to God, not to its members. And the church is valuable to God—so special that he sent his Son to die for it. Of course, it is not that we are special in ourselves—we are special because we are God's.

- **Imagine you are one of Peter's first readers—marginalized and misunderstood by your society. How would verse 9 encourage you? What dangers would it guard you against?**

Peter's message to his readers is: *Though now all you seem to experience is humiliation and shame—though those around you see you as irrelevant nobodies—you are members of a new race, royal servants of the supreme King, citizens of a divine kingdom, and residents of a heavenly city.*

Here are some dangers this encouragement might guard you against:
- giving up because the Christian life is hard.
- giving up on the church and seeking to live as a "lone ranger" Christian.
- becoming demoralized because the church is rejected by most, and seems irrelevant or offensive to them.
- becoming passive within the church—being part of it because it's necessary, but not being excited about church or serving sacrificially within church.
- becoming passive about witness—forgetting that part of our identity is to represent God to the world.

8. What is one purpose of the church, according to verse 9? How do local churches do this?

To "proclaim the excellencies of him who called you out of darkness into his marvelous light." The purpose of the church is to declare the gospel to the world. This means we are to make much of God, to pursue his fame by proclaiming his wonderful deeds—supremely, how he saves us.

Explore More

○ **Read Hosea 1 and 1 Peter 2:10. How does Peter link what has happened to these believers in Asia Minor (and in your locality today) with what God prophesied through Hosea?**

Hosea looked forward to a day when God would restore Israel after having rejected them. Because of their idolatry, God declared that he would "no more have mercy" and that Israel would now be "not my people" (Hosea 1:6, 9)—and yet that one day, "the children of Israel shall be like the sand of the sea, which cannot be measured or numbered … it shall be said to them, 'Children of the living God'" (v 10). In 1 Peter 2:10, the apostle says in effect to his readers, "Hosea was talking about you." And what is surprising is that Israel's restoration includes these Gentile Christians, scattered throughout Asia Minor. Though they were "not a people," they have become "God's people," and though they "had not received mercy," now they "have received mercy" (v 10; Hosea 2:23).

○ **How does God describes the natural state of his people ("land") in Hosea 1:2?**
As having committed "great whoredom," like an unfaithful wife. We are spiritual adulterers. (James picks up on this description and applies it to New Testament Christians in James 4:4-5.)

○ **So why is it astonishing that we should be treated as "children of the living God," who "have received mercy"?**
Because we have treated God, and continue to treat God, unfaithfully—and yet he chooses to have mercy on us through Christ, making and keeping us as his children. It is astonishing that those who are such sinners as us should be so beloved by God.

9. **What is a second purpose of the church (v 12)?**
To "keep your conduct among the Gentiles honorable"—"honorable" means "godly," so Peter is telling the church to live in such a way that God's good rule is seen by others around them. They are to display the gospel.

• **What is the aim of doing this (end of verse 12)?**
So that those around us might "glorify God on the day of visitation." The nature of the glory God will receive is unclear—it could be referring to those who have seen the good deeds of the church, have listened and responded to the message of the church, and therefore are saved and able to glorify God when Christ returns; and/or it could be referring to those who continue to reject Christ, but who must confess on the day Jesus returns in judgment that they did see his kingdom displayed in the church, and that his judgment for their rejection is just.

• **How are these two purposes linked?**
Our lives commend our message, and our message explains our lives. We display the kingdom in our lives, and we declare the kingdom with our words. So as we live our lives together as a church, unbelievers should be able to see our transformed lives and hear our transformational message, and glorify God at the final judgment. We must declare the gospel, and not ever think that social justice,

good deeds, and so on constitute our mission. But there is an equal and opposite danger—that of proclaiming the gospel without living (individually and as churches) in a way that commends that gospel.

10. **How would that prevent us fulfilling our purpose as God's church?**

Because this view means we will disengage from the world, and so we will not be in the mission field we have been called to. We cannot declare or display the gospel if no one ever sees us or hears from us! Our fight is against sin and temptation, worldliness and the devil—and that is a fight that takes place within us, not around us. So we need to ask ourselves, "Am I actually warring against my own sin as I seek to love the world and those who are still lost in darkness; or do I actually indulge my sin while looking down on or remaining aloof from the world?"

NOTE: The rest of the letter will be concerned with showing us how we can keep our conduct "honorable"—how we can live in the world without being consumed by it; how to display and declare the excellencies of God to a world that is hostile to us because it is hostile to him.

• **Why is that approach to pursuing holiness futile in any case (v 11)?**

Because our problem is not "out there," but "in here"—it is the "passions of the flesh" that war against our soul. Even if we withdraw completely from the world, our sinful desires will not be left behind. Holiness involves loving the world while we fight our sin.

11. **How is your own church both declaring and displaying the beauty of living under God's loving rule:**
   • **to one another?**
   • **to those around you?**
   • **Are you in any way at risk of prioritizing one of these but ignoring the other?**

This is an opportunity for you to discuss your own individual and church approach to the Christian life, both within the congregation and in terms of mission to the community around you. Seek to ensure the conversation is both encouraging and challenging—all our churches are capable of declaring and displaying the kingdom better, but equally all our churches will be doing one and/or the other to some extent. Praise God for what he is doing through you, and pray to God to ask him to do more through you!

12. **Share what has particularly excited you during this study about being part of the church.**

Encourage concise answers. Hopefully, your group members will have been excited by different aspects of the church's identity and mission. You might like to turn the answers they give into prayers of praise.

4

In His Footsteps

1 Peter 2:13 - 3:7

The Big Idea

We follow in Christ's footsteps by submitting to those in positions of authority, even when that involves suffering unjustly. As we do this, we enable others to see the reality and attractiveness of the Christian faith.

Summary

In this section of his letter, Peter shows us how we are to conduct ourselves when it comes to authority, and when it comes to suffering. He identifies three authorities to whom we are to "be subject," or submit: the state's authorities (2:13-17), our "masters" in our workplaces (v 18-20), and wives submitting to husbands in marriages (3:1-6). Each time, he gives a reason and a motivation, as you will see in the study. (Note that in the section on marriages, Peter speaks challengingly to husbands as well as wives, in verse 7).

In the middle of this section, Peter introduces a theme that will dominate the rest of his letter: how Christians respond when we face suffering that is as a result of our faith and is unfair. And he teaches us to see these as times when we are being called to follow in Christ's footsteps, since he suffered greatly, and totally unjustly.

The word "example" (2:21) is a word that refers to the letters children would trace in order to learn how to write. As Christians, we are called to "trace" Jesus' footsteps. Where Jesus stepped, we step, and his steps take us along the path of unjust suffering. In verses 22-25, Peter retraces Jesus' steps through the words of Isaiah. Our Master is the suffering servant; when we suffer as servants, we are following in his footsteps. We're not to compromise in our conduct to avoid suffering, nor to aggressively attack those who cause that suffering. The challenge is that at moments of unjust suffering, we discover who we truly worship—comfort or Christ.

Optional Extra

To introduce the idea of following in someone's footsteps—that is, following their example—ask two people in your group to stand opposite one another. One must copy (in mirror image, unless you want to make it really hard!) whatever the other one does.

Guidance for Questions

1. **How do you respond to the word "submit"? Is submitting a positive thing or a negative thing?**

   Depending on the individuals in your group, and your wider culture, people will respond very differently. Allow the discussion about the positivity or negativity of submission to take in differing views. Generally,

Western culture has a negative view of submission—and so Peter's teaching here will be countercultural.

NOTE: This discussion may reveal some difficult experiences from a person's past or present. Bear those in mind and walk with sensitivity as you move through each area of "being subject" that Peter covers here (i.e. government, workplace, marriage).

2. **Who are Christians to "be subject" to (2:13-14,:18; 3:1)?**
   - "Every human institution," or authority (2:13-14)—in Peter's day, the emperor and his governors. These, then, are the authorities in your nation.
   - "Your masters" (v 18). And though we are likely not servants, notice that almost immediately Peter extends his commands to servants out to all Christians: "servants" in verse 18 becomes "one" in verse 19. Since all of us are "servants" to earthly "masters" in certain contexts—especially in the workplace—all of us can apply this passage to ourselves, and live out Peter's teaching.
   - NOTE: "Servants" is literally "household slaves." You may need to explain that in the Roman Empire, slavery was different than in the modern era and the Atlantic slave trade. Slaves were often well educated. They might have served as physicians or tutors to children. Though it was difficult, slaves had the opportunity to buy their freedom. So while slavery was never

desirable, it was not as bad as we might think. The very fact that Peter addresses slaves gives them a place of dignity.
   - Wives are to submit to their husbands (3:1). Submission in marriage means to allow the husband to lead, and to follow that lead. It does not mean never to hold an opinion or take part in discussion.

- **How do you respond to these three "be subject" commands? Why?**
  This is an opportunity for you to gauge where your group may need to spend more time discussing Peter's commands here. Depending on your culture, one or other of the three "be subject" commands may be more difficult to understand or accept. Chapters 7 – 8 of *1 Peter For You* give more detailed help on the reason for and goodness of Peter's commands here.

3. **How does Peter detail what it means to "be subject" in each of these areas?**
- **2:15-17**
  - It means being good citizens (v 15-16). Freedom in Christ is not a freedom to sin (v 16). Neither is freedom in Christ a freedom from responsibility. And our responsibility to governing authorities is not merely to do no harm; our responsibility is actually to do good (v 15). "Doing good" describes a general generous posture toward others that shows itself in how we act toward them. In other words, in

any given situation, we are to seek the welfare of others.

- We "honor everyone" (v 17). Humans bear God's image, so they are to be honored. To honor someone is to treat them as valuable, as a person of worth. We treat others with the dignity due to them as God's creatures.
- We are to "love the brotherhood" (v 17)—we are not to neglect our church as we seek to serve our society.
- We are to "fear God" (v 17). We obey the authorities, but we are not in awe of them—we are in awe of God.
- Peter says that even the "emperor"—who stood at the head of a government increasingly opposed to the church—is to be honored, as a creature made in God's image and an authority placed over people by God's will.

- **2:18-19**
  - Respecting those who are in authority over us (v 18).
  - To continue to live "mindful of God"—as a Christian—when we face unjust suffering because of our faith (v 19).

- **3:2, 4**
  - "Respectful and pure conduct."
  - "A gentle and quiet spirit." It is worth defining these qualities. The word "gentle" means humble, as opposed to harsh. Sometimes it is translated "meek" and is used of Jesus, who brought his kingdom

on the earth without harshness or military force. "Quiet" has the sense of a quietness of peace, as opposed to the loudness of war. It means being a calming presence, particularly when things are or could become warlike—to calmly pursue peace while others around create war. Notice that to be gentle and quiet is not incompatible with being extroverted, talkative, humorous, enthusiastic, and so on. And notice, too, that the qualities of gentleness and quietness betray strength, not weakness.

Explore More

- ○ **Read Acts 5:17-32. How do Peter's conduct and words here help us to understand when Christians are not to "be subject to" the authorities?** Peter stood before the most powerful court in his nation—the court that had sentenced his Master to death months before—and refused to obey them by keeping quiet about Jesus: "We must obey God rather than men" (v 29). This is why they kept teaching the gospel (v 21). So when a human authority commands something that means to obey would require disobeying God, then we obey God, not men. While we are to obey all governing authorities without exception, sometimes there are exceptions to our submission.

- ○ **Can you think of examples in your own society when you might need** *respectfully to tell an authority that you "must obey God rather than men"?*

---

4. What motivations does Peter give for submitting in these three ways?

- **2:15**

  As we obey the rules of earthly governments, we provide a faithful witness to our King and true home in order to "put to silence the ignorance of foolish people." As we pay whatever taxes are due, obey the laws of the state, honor those in authority, and encourage righteousness and justice, then we will silence those who may be tempted to slander us. They may malign us for our gospel beliefs, but they will have no grounds to criticize us for our relationship to the authorities or our involvement in society.

- **2:20b**

  Suffering for doing good is "a gracious thing in the sight of God." God sees, is delighted by, and loves to reward costly faithfulness. ("Gracious thing" is literally "grace"—i.e. God responds to costly faithfulness by giving undeserved kindness.) There may be no reward for living as a Christian in your workplace from anyone else in your workplace—but there will be a reward from the Lord for living in a way that is mindful of him.

- **3:1, 4b**

  If a Christian wife is married to a non-Christian, then their conduct may win their husband to give the gospel a hearing.

  NOTE: We need to guard against two mistakes when it comes to this situation. The first is where an unbelieving husband finds that his wife tries to turn every conversation into a gospel presentation. While well-intentioned, this tends to push people away from the gospel, not draw them toward it. This is why Peter speaks of wives influencing their husbands "without a word."

  But second, this is not a call to "silent witness," where no conversation turns to Christ because the believing wife is sticking to "without a word"! Peter's thinking in this section will reach verse 15—be "prepared to make a defense to anyone who asks you for a reason for the hope that is in you.")

  Living this way is, to God, "very precious" (v 4). Just as a servant/employee who suffers unjustly can know that God sees, cares, and is pleased by their faith, so a wife who submits faithfully can know that God sees and is pleased, even if no one else appreciates her conduct and sacrifice.

5. What do you think it means for a husband to treat his wife "in an understanding way" (3:7)?

"Understanding" interprets two Greek words that are simply translated "according to knowledge." Men who understand their wives show "honor to the woman as the weaker vessel" (v 7, which simply means that, generally speaking, God created women as physically weaker than men). Most men have the potential to control their wives by sheer physical, brute strength. But again, that would be to live out the curse, rather than God's creation design. No, Christian husbands are to seek to be understanding and honoring—to lead their marriage as Christ leads his church, by loving their wives as Christ loves his people (Ephesians 5:25-33). Christian husbands are to lead their wives with an understanding that leads to a sacrificial, servant love which allows our wives to flourish and grow as disciples of Jesus under our care. That's what godly leadership does.

- **Why would this make it easier for a wife gladly to "be subject to" him?**
  Because if a wife knows that her husband is prayerfully, carefully, and sacrificially making decisions and setting directions that are aimed at being for her godliness and her good, then she can more easily gladly submit.

6. **What is the sign that a husband is loving his wife well (v 7b)? Why is this, do you think?**
   Their prayers are "not … hindered." Prayer (together and individual) flourishes in a marriage where husband and wife are in step together, and each prioritizing Christ together, and where the wife knows her husband wants her best and is doing his best to lead in that direction. There will be less annoyance and bitterness when

a husband makes an effort to understand his wife—and it is hard to pray when we are annoyed or bitter.

7. **How do each of these "be subject" commands look today, in your life?**
   Discuss how we are called to be subject in terms of authorities, workplaces, and marriages. (If you have time, discuss how the husband is commanded to live in 3:7, as well as how the wife is to live in verse 1). Try to be specific and practical in your answers ("I need to obey the speed limits" rather than "I need to be subject to the authorities") and bear in mind that obedience will look different in each person's life.

- **When is being subject in these ways hardest for you, and why? How has this passage encouraged and challenged you to submit nonetheless?**
  Remind your group that when obedience to God's commands is hard, it is a great opportunity to please him and to grow in holiness.

8. **What kind of life are we all called to live as Christians (v 21)?**
   "This"—which refers us back to verse 20, which speaks of suffering unjustly. But Peter also points us to Christ, and says that we have been called to "follow in his steps." Our life is to be the kind of life that Jesus himself lived.

9. **What example did Jesus leave for us (v 22-23)?**
   First, notice that in his life, Christ was "reviled," and he "suffered" (v 23).

So to step where Jesus stepped is to go through unjust suffering. Unjust suffering is not a sign that we've done something wrong or that God has failed us, any more than it was for Jesus. Jesus knew what he was saying when he promised a cross to every one of his followers (Mark 8:34).

Second, notice how Jesus responded to unjust suffering:

- He did not sin (1 Peter 2:22). When we suffer, that is no excuse to sin.
- He did not verbally lash out or threaten those who caused his unjust suffering (v 23). We all know the temptation to lash out verbally when wrongly accused or mistreated for no reason. But Jesus did not revile in return; when he suffered, he did not threaten. How can we actually do this, again and again and day after day? Peter tells us...
- He trusted God (v 23). Jesus entrusted himself to his Father, knowing there would be a reckoning. He cared more about the approval of his Father on that day than vindication from people in the present. The only way to fight the temptation to retaliate against our oppressors or to exact revenge is by being "mindful of God" (v 19). If we can trust God to right all wrongs, then we can face unjust suffering without retaliation because we have no need to take justice into our own hands. We can leave it in God's.

10. In his suffering, Jesus is always our example; but how is he also far more than our example (v 24-25)?

The purpose of Jesus' death was to put an end to sin and free his people to live in righteousness. By his death on the cross, Jesus paid the penalty for the sins of his people and now offers forgiveness to those who turn away from their sin and entrust themselves to him—"by his wounds [we] have been healed" (v 24). We were "straying like sheep" in this world as we followed the passions of our ignorance, but Jesus has made a way for us to return "to the Shepherd and Overseer of [our] souls" (v 25).

- **How should verses 24-25 move us to follow Jesus' example, do you think?**

Because he did all this for us. All his unjust suffering was avoidable, yet he walked through it, even through his death, in order to bear our sins, heal us, and return us to relationship with God. When we truly realize this, we follow Christ out of gratitude, suffer for him as a privilege, and remember that as God had a purpose in Christ's suffering, so he has a purpose in ours.

11. What has Peter shown us about what it will look like to worship Christ?

It will mean that we suffer, unfairly, just as Christ did. It will mean that we are subject in our societies, in our workplaces, and (if we are wives) in our marriages, even where and when that is hard or undesirable. Worshiping Christ will never be easy.

- **What else are we tempted to worship at moments of unjust suffering?**

  Think about why we opt out of unjust suffering. It may be because we value our comfort more highly than Christ; or because we value our reputation, or our wealth, or our career, or our independence.

12. **How has this passage affected your expectations of your life, and your view of suffering in your life?**

    We can tend to think that if we simply live good lives, then God is sure to bless us. Our prayers are easily dominated by pleas for God to keep us and our families safe, and make us happy by giving us all that we want or think we need. This passage should change that view of our life! We also tend to see suffering as a disaster, to be avoided at all costs, rather than as an inevitability, to be borne faithfully and responded to in a Christ-like way.

5

Christ Also Suffered
1 Peter 3:8 - 4:6

The Big Idea

Christ's pathway was through suffering to vindication and inheritance; his people's path will be the same. On our way there, we bless others, give a reason for our hope, and live by God's will, not that of the world or our own desires.

Summary

Peter's words to us in study 4—be subject, bear unjust suffering, keep your conduct honorable—are not easy to live out. Now, Peter teaches us how to persevere—how to live out his teaching not only for a few days but for a lifetime of exile, until we reach our imperishable inheritance.

And that perseverance comes from remembering where we are going as we follow Christ's steps. 3:18-22 is a very hard passage, and it is worth studying closely and reading more in-depth treatments before you come to lead the study. But it is crucial, because its central message is: We persevere even when we suffer for doing good because Jesus has already walked the road marked with righteous suffering—and it was the pathway to his vindication and glory. Christ suffered for us, and like us—and he then rose from the dead to declare his victory to his spiritual enemies and to rule all things.

So he is the "hope" that we have, and

that we are to be prepared to speak of when asked or attacked (v 15-16). And, since we know that we are heading for a day of judgment when we will be saved, we do not live as we used to, and as others still do—we seek to think like him, and live for him (4:1-2).

Optional Extra

Watch a clip of the TV reality show *Preachers of L.A.*, which follows Californian prosperity-gospel preachers, including their opulent lifestyles. Discuss how their version of "Christianity" compares with the picture of the Christian life Peter has been laying out in his letter so far. Ask your group how they might, even while rejecting this prosperity gospel, in fact have more in common with it than they do with Peter's view of Christianity, in their expectations about life and the way they make decisions day by day. This will lead you into question 1.

Guidance for Questions

1. **What do you think they would conclude that the Christian life was like, and what conduct would they think was most important to Christians?**
   - **Now imagine we give the same researcher a month to read the New Testament. Do you think they would change their conclusions at all? If so, how?**

   There are, of course, no right or wrong answers to these questions. But I suspect that the answer to each would not have a great deal in common.

Western Christianity is often compromised by materialism, consumerism, and prosperity. New Testament Christianity, as we have been seeing in 1 Peter, is marked by a joyful and faithful endurance through many obstacles and much opposition.

To make this point, you could read to your group Acts 14:22; Romans 8:17; and Philippians 1:29; and ask what we do with these verses. Often we do nothing with them, except to gently, quietly ignore them or apply them to Christians facing persecution elsewhere. If so, we are not living the Christianity of the New Testament.

You could return to this question at the end of the study, and ask your group: what changes might we need to make as individuals and as a church so that a researcher would make the same conclusions about the Christian life from observing our conduct as they would from reading the New Testament?

2. **How should we live (v 8-12)?**
   - Have unity of mind (v 8)
   - Sympathy (v 8)
   - Brotherly love (v 8)
   - A tender heart (v 8)
   - A humble mind (v 8)

   In one sense, these five are all one command: a command to love other Christians sympathetically and compassionately. In this section, Peter is transitioning from talking about submitting to talking about suffering—and it is hard to be loving when you are suffering.

- "Do not repay evil for evil … but on the contrary, bless" (v 9). We are called not only not to curse, but actively to bless.
- Don't use your tongues for evil or deceit (v 10). Again, this is very hard when you are suffering or struggling.
- Do good; seek peace (v 11). In every situation we pursue peace, even with those who are treating us badly.

- **For each command, think of a practical way in which this is different than how we would naturally conduct ourselves.**

  For instance, when we are maligned or verbally attacked, it is easy to use our words to fight back (evil) or to duck out (deceit). That is our natural reaction; but Peter here calls us to do neither, and instead to pursue peace.

3. **"Obtain" (v 9) is better translated "inherit." Reread 1:3-5. What do we know awaits us, and how does this enable us to suffer and to bless?**

   Our future inheritance, which is imperishable, undefiled, and unfading, guaranteed by Christ's resurrection. Peter is saying, *As you seek to bless even as you suffer, you can know that you are walking toward your inheritance.* It is as you live the Christian life that you can look forward to life with Christ. We suffer well now not in order to be a Christian but because we are a Christian (which is why "obtain" is an unhelpful translation)—

because we know our inheritance awaits us.

4. **Why do Christians need neither to fear nor be troubled by those who harm them (3:13-14)?**

   Because Christians are assured of the blessing of their future inheritance, there is nothing anyone can do to us, because there is no way anyone can take that from us; so, in the final analysis, a Christian has nothing to fear. That means that there is no amount of harm that anyone can do to us that will deprive us of our inheritance—not even death. We will likely suffer as Christians in this world, but that suffering is slight and temporary compared to the eternal inheritance that awaits us. The worst thing that can happen to us is that we die and receive our promised inheritance.

- **What should they do instead (v 15-16)?**
  - "Honor Christ the Lord as holy" (v 15)—acknowledge his lordship and goodness, and so submit to him that our actions are directed by what pleases him. We are to be far more in awe of him and care far more about his approval than we are to be in awe or seek the approval of other people.
  - Be prepared to give a "reason for the hope that is in you" (v 15). Peter is preparing us for the possibility that in the midst of Christian suffering, our persecutors may ask us to give a reason for the hope that we have—that is, why we believe what

we believe. It is this hope that frees us to be bold and courageous in the face of persecution.

- "Do it with gentleness and respect" (v 15). When attacked, we are to respond without harshness or superiority.

- **Why?**
So that those who hate the way Christians live "may be put to shame" (v 16); they may be either ashamed now, and therefore repentant and placing their trust in Christ as their hope, or ashamed when Christ returns and they see who is the King and how they have treated him and his people.

5. **How would your life, conduct, and words be different if you really did not fear anything because you knew that the worst that can happen cannot happen—that you cannot lose God's love for you?**
Encourage your group to be specific, and give them time individually to write down some specific aspects of their life that would change if they had this attitude, before asking them to share. You may like to pause and pray about the answers people give.

6. **What do verses 15-16 teach us about how to share our faith faithfully and effectively?**
- Our heart attitude is where it starts. If we "honor Christ the Lord as holy"—if he is who we most esteem and obey—then we will live differently, which will cause

others to notice and ask (possibly aggressively).

- Be prepared to answer. We need to have a "defense" ready—to have an answer to the questions we are asked that points to our "hope"—in other words, Christ.

- Be gentle and respectful. Our tone and attitude must not be those of someone looking down on another.

- **Which aspect do you find hardest, and why? What encouragement or help do you need?**
If there are prayer needs or training needs (e.g. in apologetics), make sure you follow up on this, either yourself or by passing it to someone in your church's pastoral team.

Explore More

○ *Respond to one (or more) of these statements in a way that gives a reason for the hope that you have (in other words, that talks about Jesus), and does so "with gentleness and respect."*

○ *Christianity is irrelevant.*

○ *Science has disproved the Bible.*

○ *A good God would not allow suffering.*

○ *It is arrogant to say that Christianity is the only right religion.*

○ *The Bible's teaching on sexual morality is outdated and bigoted.*
This section tests your group's preparedness. Split members into pairs and have them speak to one another about one each (or more) of the

statements. Bear in mind that verses 15-16 tell us that we need to…

- *have an answer.*
- *point to Christ in our answer.*
- *be gentle and respectful (so our tone is not argumentative and we respect the question and the questioner).*

Most of us struggle with at least one, and often all three, of these!

NOTE: Verses 18-22 are extremely complex. You will find more detail of, and the reasons for, my position in *1 Peter For You*, pages 131-138. Remember to major on the major point, rather than being sidetracked by less crucial issues. The point of these verses is to show the pathway Jesus followed, and to assure us that if we are on that path, it will lead us to where he is.

7. What event do these verses begin with, and what event do they end with (v 18, 22)?

- v 18: Jesus' death.
- v 22: Jesus' ascension and exaltation—his being given the most authoritative place in the universe ("at the right hand of God"), with the entire spiritual world bowing to him.

8. What did Jesus' death achieve (v 18)? How does this encourage us to stay faithful when we suffer?

Jesus' death was able to "bring us to God," because it was the one-time suffering of a righteous man in the place of unrighteous people.

Jesus walked the path marked with righteous suffering all the way to his death on the cross, and in doing so, he blazed the trail for us to follow. His cross opened the way to relationship with God eternally. This encourages us because…

- his death means that we can know with certainty that we will one day be with God, in that glorious inheritance.
- his death, followed by his exaltation, shows us the template of Christian living—it is very hard, and then beyond death it is absolutely wonderful.

9. How does knowing what Jesus did after his resurrection (v 19) and where Jesus is now (v 22) encourage us to stay faithful when we suffer?

Jesus is supreme over everything, both in the physical and the spiritual creation. Even the demonic realm is under Jesus' authority.

10. So, as we look back to our baptism, what are we meant to remember that we can look forward to?

Salvation from judgment. A day is coming when God will destroy the ungodly, as he did in Noah's time by means of the flood (see 2 Peter 3:5-7). Baptism pictures this future judgment, and pictures us coming through it, as we come up out of the water, to enjoy glory with Christ.

- **How does this encourage us to remain faithful when we suffer?**

Because we know that Christ has

suffered in our place so that we will not have to suffer God's judgment. Our faithful suffering now is hard, but we will not face suffering on the final day.

11. **How should we think and live (v 1-2)?**

    • *Think*: We must "arm [ourselves] with the same way of thinking" as Christ (v 1), who was willing to suffer because he knew that this was his path to vindication and glory. We are to make our perspectives and our expectations line up with Christ's—to remember that suffering achieves God's purposes and to remember that beyond it lies resurrection and our inheritance.

    • NOTE: "Ceased from sin" (v 1) does not mean we will be perfect in this life, but that we have ceased to allow sin to define or drive us (as we see in verse 2).

    • *Live*: We live for the rest of this life on earth ("the time in the flesh") not "for human passions" but "for the will of God" (v 2). We do not live just as we want to, or as others expect us to—we seek to follow the will of God in all that we do.

• **Why will this make life harder, not easier (v 3-4)?**

  Because those around us live in a very different way, since they follow "human passions" (v 2—Peter gives a list of some behaviors this leads to in verse 3). This means that our lifestyles are different from the way most people live their lives—we

seem strange, and "they malign [us]" (v 4). Our old friends will mock or disown us. Those we would like to be our friends will not want to know us. Living for the will of God is more joyful, but also more difficult and costly, because the world will no longer love us.

• **What can we remember when living "for the will of God" is hard (v 5-6)?**

  • Judgment is coming (v 5). Everyone will have to give an account for how they lived in God's world and what they said to and about God's people.

  • Salvation is coming (v 6). This verse is complex. Everyone is "dead"—and everyone, including Christians, will be "judged in the flesh" (we will die)—but those who trust the gospel that has been preached to them will "live in the spirit the way God does"—in other words (as in 3:18), be resurrected to the realm of the Spirit in a spiritual, incorruptible body. So Peter is simply saying that the gospel we believe means we know that we will be saved when judgment arrives—we have hope beyond now.

12. **Paul told some young Christians, "Through many tribulations we must enter the kingdom of God" (Acts 14:22). How is this verse a good summary of what Peter has taught us here?**

  Our life will be like Christ's life: suffering (tribulations) and then enjoying resurrection life in the kingdom of God. It will be like this because he has walked this way before us, suffering in our place to "bring us to God" (1 Peter 3:18). So we will face evil and be called to bless; we will suffer for righteousness' sake; we will be attacked and will need to give a reason for our hope; we will be maligned by those who are surprised that we don't live as they do. These are some of the tribulations that following in Christ's steps brings; and Peter has taught us to look beyond them, to our inheritance, knowing that where Christ is now, we will one day be.

6

Stand Firm, for the End Is at Hand
1 Peter 4:7 - 5:14

The Big Idea
Because we know that the end—Jesus' return and the arrival of our inheritance—is near, we keep loving one another, suffer joyfully, submit to our elders as they lead us, and stand firm in God's grace.

Summary
This final study aims to take you through the end of the letter, but also to enable your group to sum up, reflect on, and apply to themselves the overall message of the whole letter.

In many ways, the "summary verse" of the letter is 5:12, where Peter says he has written about "the true grace of God" so that his readers will "stand firm in it." In this last section, he exhorts us to stand firm because "the end of all things is at hand" (4:7). We need to live remembering that Jesus' return to judge and bring us to our future inheritance is near, and could be today. Peter says that knowing this means we need to…

- love one another earnestly and practically (4:7-11).
- suffer without surprise, and with joy (v 12-19).
- submit to the leadership of our God-given elders so that we will not wander off (5:1-5).
- humble ourselves to place ourselves into God's care, resist the devil, and remember that our suffering is for "a little while" compared to our eternal inheritance (v 6-11).

Optional Extra
Watch some footage from the Comrades Marathon (a 56-mile ultramarathon

in South Africa)—for instance: youtube.com/watch?v=JFjssNLgvFk.

Talk about how the runners must feel halfway through. Would they be surprised by the pain? Why / why not? Why do they keep going? (Because they know that keeping going, though painful, means they will reach the finish.)

Then talk about how the runners must feel at the finish—and note that the difficulty of the race is what makes the feeling at the finish all the more sweet.

Link to this after question 4 or 5. The Christian life is painful, and so we should not be surprised when our lives are painful. But we can still rejoice, rather than despair or quit, because we know that there is a finish line and we are excited about what lies at that finish line.

Guidance for Questions

1. **If you knew the world would end in 24 hours, how would you spend your last day? Who with? And how would you feel?**
   Your group may choose to answer this seriously or humorously, but the point is that knowing that the end of the world is very close would dominate and direct everything. And Peter says in 4:7, "The end of all things is at hand."

2. **What does Peter remind us of (v 7)?**
   "The end of all things is at hand"— the day when this world as we know it ends as Jesus returns is near.

• **Read 1:3-4, 7. How do you feel about knowing this day is "at hand"?**
The end is when our living hope will be realized and when we will receive our imperishable, undefiled, unfading inheritance. It is when we will stand with Jesus Christ, and hear his words of praise because we have kept going in genuine, joyful faith despite all our trials. So surely, the closer that day is, the more joyful we will be. It is the day when everything we have looked forward to will arrive, and when losing things in order to live by faith will be proved to have been worth it. And it could come very soon. How exciting—how confidence-building!

3. **What implications will knowing that this day is coming have (4:7-11)?**
   • We will be "self-controlled" (which might helpfully be translated, "Keep your head"). We are to be clear-headed—and we are not to panic, but to pray (v 7).
   • NOTE: Peter uses the phrase "one another" in verses 8, 9, and 10—he is teaching that knowing the end is at hand has implications for how we live our lives together as church.
   • Most of all, we will love each other (v 8), forgiving others' sins rather than allowing them to provoke divisive conflict (see Proverbs 10:12).
   • We will show hospitality to one another without grumbling (1 Peter 4:9). We need consciously to see our homes as gifts to be opened and shared, and we need to ask

God's help to do this joyfully, not grumblingly.

- We will use our gifts to serve others (v 10). Every Christian has received the "grace" (kindness) of a God-given gift. We are stewards of those gifts—they have been given to us to use wisely in order to "serve one another," be it through teaching or through practical ministries (v 11).

4. In the face of this "fiery trial," what should we not be (v 12)?

We should not be surprised. Peter says "when" Christian suffering comes, not if. Christian suffering is an inevitable reality for anyone who lives a truly Christian life. So we should not be surprised when we experience it. Suffering for our faith is not a sign that things have gone wrong, but that they are going right.

○ *OPTIONAL: Why does verse 19 say Christians suffer? How does this help us not to respond with surprise?*

Suffering occurs "according to God's will." God is using our suffering for our good and for our godliness. God never promises to take us around suffering or out of suffering, but rather, to lead us through suffering. So we should not be surprised—it is his will that we suffer, in order to show the genuineness of our faith and to help us to grow more like Christ.

- **What should we do, and why (v 13-16, 19)?**

Rejoice! We do this because...

- we are sharing in Christ's sufferings—we are suffering for our faith as our Lord suffered for his (v 13).

- we know we will one day be in glory—we can enjoy this truth even as life is painful (v 13).

- we know the "Spirit of glory," who directed and equipped Christ (see Isaiah 11), now rests on us (1 Peter 4:14).

- we know we need never be ashamed of knowing Jesus, even when we are mocked for it (v 16)—suffering for Christ is an opportunity to live for and speak of "that name," bringing glory to God.

- we get on with "doing good" because we trust that God is our "faithful Creator" (v 19). Because we can trust him to do what is best, and we know that he is in charge as the Maker of all things, we can live in a godly, costly way, rather than taking matters into our own hands or doing what is safest.

Explore More

○ *What has already begun "at the household of God"—the church (v 17)?*

Judgment. Somehow, the end-time judgment that all people will face (v 5) has already begun even now in the church.

○ *Read Matthew 25:31-46. Who is being separated from whom here, and when?*

Sheep from goats—the righteous

(Christ-trusting) people and the un-righteous (non-Christ-trusting) people. And it happens when the King—Jesus—returns to bring his kingdom.

o **How does suffering in this life separate those two groups within the visible church?**

Suffering proves the genuineness (or otherwise) of someone's faith. It reveals those who are God's people as he brings them through it trusting him, and exposes those who are not really his people as they stop trusting him. This latter group were members of the visible but church, but not true members of God's people.

o **How does this help us understand what Peter means in 1 Peter 4:17?**

Suffering divides sheep and goats—it makes plain what the verdict will be at the final judgment. So in this sense, that judgment is already underway in the church through Christian suffering. As Peter adds in the form of a question, if this suffering is faced by God's people, imagine how terrible it will be one day for those who are not God's people.

5. **How has the whole of 1 Peter helped you to be neither surprised about nor despairing at the reality that the Christian life is a life of suffering?**

• **How has it helped you to respond to that suffering with joy?**

Give your group time to flick their eyes over the letter, picking out verses or passages that enable us to suffer well as Christians, and explaining how the truths they've picked out change our attitude to trials. Make sure you discuss how 1 Peter helps us actively and positively to be joyful, rather than only to avoid the negatives of surprise or despair when we face a time of suffering.

6. **Who has God given to his church to help Jesus' "sheep" (v 1-2a)?**

Elders (v 1): these people are "shepherds" of a part of "the flock of God" (v 2a).

NOTE: In the New Testament, these under-shepherds are referred to as either elders, overseers, or pastors; the terms are interchangeable. Today, we call them pastors, or ministers, or elders, or vicars.

7. **What should elders do, and remember (v 2-4)?**

• Shepherd the flock (v 2)—lead, protect, and provide, just as 1st-century shepherds did.

• Exercise oversight (v 2)—so elders must lead and direct. They have genuine authority.

• Lead willingly, not "under compulsion" (v 2).

• Pastor eagerly, not for their own gain (v 2). Put simply, elders must not be in it for their own gain (financial, reputational, or other). The motivation is to be caring for the flock, not paying the bills or looking good.

• Be an example, not a dominator (v 3). Faithful shepherds don't lord it over others; they serve those under their care. (See Jesus' words on this subject in Mark 10:42-44.)

- Remember the reward: a crown like the crown of leaves given to athletic and military victors, but a crown that is "unfading" (1 Peter 5:4). When elders serve at great cost and feel burdened or burned out, and receive little or no thanks, they need to look up and look ahead to the joy they will experience when they receive their unfading crown from the Lord.

- **What should church members do, and remember (v 5)?**

  As church members, Peter calls us to "be subject to the elders." Assuming our elders are striving to be the kind of elders Peter describes in verses 2-4, we need to follow their lead, speak loyally of them, pray for and support them—and do so when they make a decision we do not understand.

8. **What should our attitude be toward...**

- **God?**

  Humility (v 6). We entrust ourselves into his hands even as we suffer, knowing that he is mighty, that he cares for us, and that he is leading us toward our inheritance. But it does require humility to allow God to be in charge, and to rejoice in the truth that he is, even when we do not understand what he is doing. We need to remember that he is the God of all kindness ("grace"), who has called us to "eternal glory" (v 10).

- **the devil?**

  We must resist him (v 9), because we know he seeks to "devour" our faith (v 8). This means that our attitude is to be neither obsessive nor dismissive. The devil is real, and we must be ready for his attacks; but he is defeated, and therefore we are able to "stand firm" (v 12) and not give in to his temptations.

- **our suffering?**

  - There is no safer place to be than under God's mighty hand (v 6)—and suffering in this life does not mean that we are not in his hands.
  - Suffering is a time when the devil will seek to devour us—so suffering is a time to be particularly "sober-minded" and "watchful" (v 8).
  - Suffering is normal for Christians (v 9)—we are not going through anything that other Christians round the world don't face, and stay faithful in.
  - Our suffering is only for "a little while" (v 10) compared to the "eternal glory" we have ahead of us.

9. **Flick your eyes over the letter. How would it have encouraged the Christians to "stand firm"?**

  Let your group make suggestions, but verses you might look at include...

  - 1:1
  - 1:2
  - 1:3-5
  - 1:6-9
  - 1:18-19
  - 2:4-6

- 2:21
- 3:18-22
- 4:4-6

- How would it have showed them what it looks like each day to "stand firm"?
  - 1:13-16
  - 1:22
  - 2:1-3
  - 2:9
  - 2:11-12
  - 2:13, 18
  - 3:1, 7
  - 3:8-9
  - 4:1-3

10. Share how the letter has encouraged you to "stand firm" as a Christian.
- Share one or two things that the Spirit has been prompting you to change in your thoughts or actions as you have studied 1 Peter.

  These questions are opportunities for your group to spend time reflecting on how God has been speaking to them in their particular situations during your time studying this letter. (There will be an opportunity to pray for one another at the end of the session.)

11. This guide is titled *Living Well on the Way Home*. Use this letter to sum up in one sentence each...
- what is exciting about our future home.
- how we can live well, in God's sight, on our way there.

  Ask your group to write their own answers first, before comparing and contrasting them. Use the sentences to direct your prayer time at the end of the session, before moving on to pray for the specific answers you shared for question 10.

Go Deeper with the Expository Guide to

1 Peter

by Juan R. Sanchez Jr.

Less academic than a traditional commentary, this expository guide by Juan R. Sanchez Jr. takes you through Peter's first letter verse by verse — exploring its message of joy and hope in a hostile world.

This flexible resource can enrich your personal devotions, help you lead small-group studies, or aid your sermon preparations.

Explore the God's Word For You series

thegoodbook.com/for-you
thegoodbook.co.uk/for-you
thegoodbook.com.au/for-you

Explore the Whole Range

Old Testament, including:

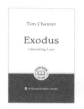 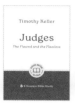 

New Testament, including:

 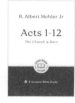 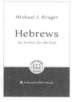

Topical, including:

   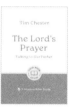

Flexible and easy to use, with over 50 titles available,
Good Book Guides are perfect for both groups and individuals.

thegoodbook.com/gbgs
thegoodbook.co.uk/gbgs
thegoodbook.com.au/gbgs

God's Word For You

Accessible Commentaries That Everyone Can Enjoy

Old Testament, including:

New Testament, including:

  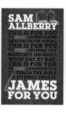 

Less academic than a traditional commentary, these expository guides take you verse by verse through books of the Bible in an accessible, applied way. These flexible resources can enrich your personal devotions, help you lead small-group studies, or aid your sermon preparations.

Use with accompanying Good Book Guides to study these books of the Bible in small groups.

thegoodbook.com/for-you

thegoodbook.co.uk/for-you

thegoodbook.com.au/for-you

BIBLICAL | RELEVANT | ACCESSIBLE

At The Good Book Company we are dedicated to helping Christians and local churches grow. We believe that God's growth process always starts with hearing clearly what he has said to us through his timeless and flawless word—the Bible.

Ever since we opened our doors in 1991, we have been striving to produce resources that are biblical, relevant, and accessible. By God's grace, we have grown to become an international publisher, encouraging ordinary Christians of every age and stage and every background and denomination to live for Christ day by day and equipping churches to grow in their knowledge of God, their love for one another, and the effectiveness of their outreach.

Call one of our friendly team for a discussion of your needs or visit one of our local websites for more information on the resources and services we provide.

Your friends at The Good Book Company

thegoodbook.com | thegoodbook.co.uk
thegoodbook.com.au | thegoodbook.co.nz
thegoodbook.co.in